Primary School A for a Just World

Edited by Gordon Lamont

First published in Great Britain in 2008

Society for Promoting Christian Knowledge
36 Causton Street
London SW1P 4ST

and

Christian Aid
35 Lower Marsh
London SE1 7RL

The authors and publishers have made every effort to ensure that the external website and email addresses included in this book are correct and up to date at the time of going to press. The author and publisher are not responsible for the content, quality or continuing accessibility of the sites.

Scriptures marked GNB are quoted from the Good News Bible, published by The Bible Societies/HarperCollins Publishers Ltd UK, copyright © American Bible Society, 1966, 1971, 1976, 1992, 1994.

Scripture quotations marked NIV are from the HOLY BIBLE, NEW INTERNATIONAL VERSION, copyright © 1973, 1978, 1984, International Bible Society. Used by permission of Hodder & Stoughton Ltd, a member of the Hodder Headline Plc Group.

Scripture quotations marked ICB are from the International Children's Bible, New Century Version (Anglicized Edition) 1991 copyright © by Word (UK) Ltd, Milton Keynes, England. Used by permission.

British Library Cataloguing-in-Publication Data
A catalogue record for this book is available from the British Library

ISBN 978–0–281–06014–6

10 9 7 6 5 4 3 2 1

Typeset by PDQ Typesetting Ltd, Newcastle-under-Lyme
Printed in Great Britain by Ashford Colour Press

Produced on paper from sustainable forests

Contents

Contributors and acknowledgements

Gordon Lamont is a former editor of the website <www.assemblies. org.uk>, which provides high-quality, instant access primary and secondary school assemblies for teachers and others leading collective worship. He is the author of several books, including *The Creative Teacher* (Arts Council, 2005), *The Assemblies Resource Book* and *Assembly Resources through the Year* (SPCK, 2001 and 2003).

Many of the assemblies in this book have been adapted from original assemblies written by the following authors on behalf of Christian Aid:

Jenny Baker: 'Freedom' (p. 22) and 'Big fat juicy snails – yum!' (p. 69)
Julia Bracewell: 'Real life magic' (p. 92)
Katie Duckworth and **Judy Rogers:** 'Community of hope' (p. 108)
Pippa Durn: 'It can start with me' (p. 7), 'Christmas: gifts, giving goats and gratitude' (p. 30), 'Football mad – mad football!' (p. 40), 'Water' (p. 75), 'Losing everything – and still there's hope' (p. 115) and 'Tomato' (p. 82)
Don Harrison: 'Helping other' (p. 98)
Beverly Hulme: 'It's all in the mix!' (p. 34) and 'Wiggly worms and fertilized food' (p. 62)
Peter Lockyer: 'Red hot chillies, red hot experts!' (p. 87)
Hilary Macmillan: 'Disaster!' (p. 49
Judy Rogers: 'Far from home' (p. 132)
Sophie Shirt: 'Development – change for the better' (p. 2) and 'Peace on earth?' (p. 138)
Daniel Sinclair: 'How much is a person worth?' (p. 126)
Angela Summer and **Maggie Lunan:** 'Landmine hero' (p. 143)

Versions of the stories in 'Kylie's dream' (p. 15) and 'Cilla recycled' (p. 154), by Gordon Lamont, first appeared on the BBC School Radio Assembly programme *Together*.

Foreword

Christian Aid was created in 1945 as a response of the churches in the UK and Ireland to the aftermath of the Second World War. Over 60 years on, we work in some of the world's poorest communities in more than 50 countries. We act where the need is greatest, regardless of race or religion, helping people to tackle the problems they face and build the life they deserve. This work is done through 600 partners – local organizations on the ground who know how to deliver the real, practical benefits that people need. At home and overseas, we campaign to change the structures that keep people poor, challenging inequality and injustice.

Around the world 1.3 billion people live in extreme poverty; 800 million people go to bed hungry every single day. And 12 million children will die this year before their fifth birthday. It needn't be like this. We can hope for a better world, where everyone lives a full life, free from poverty. We believe that we have the power to turn that hope into action and this book is a part of that vision.

Our education work has showed us time and time again that children have an innate sense of fairness and a strong reaction to injustice. School assemblies and the classroom-based activities that grow out of them provide a marvellous opportunity to encourage children to think about development issues and to harness their sense that the world does not have to be such an unjust place; that they themselves can play an integral role in bringing about a fairer world.

I hope that this book will play its part in bringing development issues to life for primary school pupils, helping them to engage and make a difference.

DR DALEEP MUKARJI
Director of Christian Aid

How to use this book

You're a busy teacher or other assembly leader. You want your assemblies to be memorable, often fun, always lively and thought-provoking. You want them to work for the range of abilities, developmental stage and age of the children sitting in front of you. You want to meet the government's requirements and you want to do all of this in a way that is relevant and meaningful to children of all faiths and cultural backgrounds as they look to you with expectation ... Not much to ask, is it?

This book will help! The 30 assemblies with classroom activities presented here have been written to help teachers and other assembly leaders address the often tricky questions that development issues present us with: how can I get this complex situation across, will I oversimplify, and do I really know what I'm talking about anyway?

The core material comes from the extensive work that Christian Aid undertakes all around the world and most assemblies are based on the experiences of particular people, often children. The assemblies are marked as suitable for Key Stage 1, Key Stage 2, and Whole School, but to some extent these are artificial demarcations: you'll certainly find plenty in the Whole School assemblies that can readily be adapted for Key Stage 1, and similarly the Whole School assemblies contain much that will work well with Key Stage 2. In some cases the same story or situation is used for Key Stages 1 and 2 but with a different emphasis appropriate to their developmental stage and curriculum requirement. So take what we offer and adapt and expand in any way that is useful, making the ideas work for your children and their situation.

The assemblies are grouped in five sections:

Section 1: Development: the BIG PICTURE
Section 2: Food, water and shelter for all
Section 3: Children
Section 4: War and peace
Section 5: Environmental issues

Again, you will find that these groupings are not mutually exclusive, as a story about a family in wartime is also a story about children and an assembly about environmental issues may also be about food, water and shelter for all. We hope that the categories provide a useful starting point when choosing which material to use and when, but they need be no more than that.

Personal stories

In some cases, because stories and events move on, you may find that the specific instances of a war zone or a particular development issue are no longer current, but the stories of change and development, and the needs and aspirations of the people involved, will always be pertinent, and most of all to your participating audience of children. In many ways they will do your work for you as they find inspiration in stories of hope and change, anger at injustice and a keen sense of what is fair.

Classroom activities

Following each assembly there are four or five ideas for classroom activities. It is intended that these should be adapted to fit individual circumstances, curriculum-based work and, not least, teacher style. Do take what is useful and ignore the rest! In some cases there are photocopiable worksheets available. If you photocopy these at 141% (enlarging from A5 to A4) they will fit an A4 page.

Making a difference

As children become engaged with the issues explored in this book they may want to do something about what they discover. One traditional response is to raise money (see page x) but it's important to remember that this isn't the only way that we can act to make a difference. Giving money can help alleviate the symptoms of poverty. But if we are to end poverty then we must attack its roots. This is because in order to change people's lives we need to change the systems which lock them into poverty. Often this will involve calling on governments to change the way they behave so that those systems are changed. Campaigning like this has made a big difference historically – just think of the abolition of slavery or more recently the campaign to cancel poor countries' debt. One way to involve children in this is to get them to write letters or create a petition to the Prime Minister about a specific poverty issue. They can tell the Prime Minister how this makes them feel (for example, hearing about a seven-year-old in Bangladesh who cannot attend school) and they should include a specific request to the government to do something about it. Usually they'll get a response which is not only exciting but is also a good way of showing children how democracy works – that we have the power to call on our leaders to act.

Fund-raising

One of the ways children can make a difference is by raising money. I am constantly impressed by the generosity of children as shown in the Blue Peter appeals or in Christian Aid or other charitable fund-raising. We should never forget that when a child gives 50p (€0.60 or 60 eurocents) towards a fairer world, this is like you or me giving £50 (€60) or more – how many of us would do that spontaneously? But although it is good to give, the real educational and life-enhancing value comes from the wonderful and inventive ways that children engage in to *raise* money, and the sense of teamwork and joint achievement that comes from a sponsored sporting event, an expressive arts production or any one of a number of creative (and often refreshingly daft) fund-raising ideas – and many parents report that children show a budding entrepreneurial streak as they persuade the adults to dig just that bit deeper!

Fund-raising can be a valuable educational experience as children think about planning a programme that utilizes all the talents in the class with a focus on:

- Who are they going to raise money for?
- What are they going to do?
- How will the money be collected (including thinking about adult supervision, for example)?
- How will they publicize the event?

The assembly **Kylie's dream** (pages 15–21) touches on this instinct to make a practical difference. It also features some ideas that others have used to raise money and have fun too.

Fund-raising, however, is not the purpose of this book. Understanding, empathy and, yes, even entertainment (for who wants to experience a dull assembly ever again!) are key to a successful assembly and are the focus of *Assemblies for a Just World*.

GORDON LAMONT

Section 1
Development:
the BIG PICTURE

DEVELOPMENT –
CHANGE FOR THE BETTER

Suitable for KS1

 Aims

To introduce the concept of development using simple terms and examples.

 Preparation and materials

- Everyday items for the quiz.
- You will need a cuddly toy that you have named.
- Optional: There is a very simple song, sung to the tune of 'Frère Jacques'.
- If time allows you might also like to include a version of the 'Action story' in **Class activities** below this assembly.

 Assembly

1. Begin by saying that you have a very difficult quiz to start the assembly. Hold up a pencil and ask for 'hands up' for children to say what it is. Do the same with a piece of paper, a bag, a book and/or any other everyday objects.

    Admit that it wasn't so difficult after all. Who thinks it's easy to name things – to say what they're called?

2. As they've done so well, say that you're going to make the next question a bit more difficult. Produce your cuddly toy and ask what it is. Agree that it is a toy dog/cat/fox, but what is it called – does anyone know?

    Tell the children the name you've given the toy (you could explain why if appropriate), and explain that some things have a special name, a name that you give them. Ask for examples such as their own toys and pets; include the children's own names given them by their parents.

3. Say that you have a special name for '9 March' (replace with the date of your birthday). Can anyone guess why? You call it 'My birthday'. Take a few 'My birthday' dates from the children.

4. Talk about the name of the school – why is it called what it is?

5. Now tell the children that you know of a school called '4th of April'. Can they guess why? Value all suggestions and then explain that it's a school in Angola, which is a country in southern Africa – a long way away! It was named after the day that Angolans stopped fighting each other and made peace. This was such an important and happy day that everyone wants to remember it. Including the children of the 4th of April School.

6. Optional: You could teach this simple song to the tune of 'Frère Jacques':

> Fourth of April, fourth of April,
> day of peace, day of peace.
> Remember fourth of April, remember fourth of April,
> day of peace, day of peace.

7. Finish by saying that you have one more word to think about. It's a long word: 'development'. It means things changing for the better. Explain that changing things for the better can work right the way around the world! Some of the money for the 4th of April School came from people in this country who wanted to help the children of Angola. Money like this is a kind of 'magic money' because once the people have the school they can do their own development – changing things for the better through learning.

 Time for reflection

What does development mean? It means …
Change for the better … When a war ends … When children have a new school to go to … When hungry people can grow their own food …
What development will you see today? What changes will you make – a new friend, learn new things, play a new game?

Prayer

Dear God,
We thank you for the 4th of April School,
named after the day when the war stopped in Angola.
Thank you for development – change for the better –
    wherever it happens.
Amen.

 Class activities

1 Singing

Practise the 4th of April song, perhaps adding actions. Can the children suggest new words for the song, based around dates or special days such as their birthday, or a festival day?

2 Action story

Use this action story exercise adapted from the KS2 assembly **Peace on earth?** (pages 138–42) to help children understand the value and importance of the 4th of April School. Explain that before the 4th of April School was built the children had their lessons outside. Ask the children to make noises and actions to show the following:

- **hot sun** beating down on their heads (sheltering under hands, flapping hands in front of face, sighing)
- **heavy rain** pouring down (fingertips drumming on floor to make rain sound, covering head with hands)
- **dust** blowing in their faces (hands in front of face, swishing sound of dusty wind)
- **sitting** on uncomfortable stones (fidgeting!).

Explain that you'd like the children to do the actions every time you say the words: 'hot sun', 'heavy rain', 'dust', 'sitting'.

This is the story of a boy called Eduardo. There has been a war in Angola in Africa where Eduardo lives but now, at last, the war is over and Eduardo can go back to school.
But look: the school is gone! It was destroyed in the

fighting. Now Eduardo has to have his lessons under the **hot sun**, and the **heavy rain**. There's **dust** everywhere and all the pupils are **sitting** on the hard, rocky ground.

Slowly the new school is being built but while this is happening Eduardo and his friends still have their lessons under the **hot sun**, and the **heavy rain**. The **dust** is everywhere and all the pupils are **sitting** on the hard, rocky ground.

Now the school is finished, but what shall they call it? Someone says, 'Let's call it the 4th of April School, because that's the day the fighting ended.'

Everyone agrees. All the children love their new school. Especially as they no longer have to have their lessons in the **hot sun**, and the **heavy rain**, with **dust** everywhere and all the pupils **sitting** on the hard, rocky ground.

You could expand this to include actions such as the children returning and seeing the space where their school was, rebuilding the school, and celebrating their new 4th of April School.

English, Drama, Citizenship

3 Thinking about development

Ask the children about the word 'development' – can they remember what it means? What development (change for the better) did the children who went to the 4th of April School find? What kind of development will the children experience today – how will things change for the better?

Are there things that they can do to produce changes for the better? You're looking for simple responses such as 'be kind to people', 'share more', 'make a new friend', etc. Ask them to write the word 'Development' at the top of a piece of paper and then write a sentence about what they are going to do today to help change things for the better.

Citizenship, PSHE, English

4 Development across the world

Remind the children of this part of the assembly:

Explain that changing things for the better can work right

the way around the world! Some of the money for the 4th of April School came from people in this country who wanted to help the children of Angola. Money like this is a kind of 'magic money' because once the people have the school they can do their own development – changing things for the better through learning.

Ask what ideas the children have for development work across the world; what changes for the better would they like to see?

PSHE, Citizenship, Spoken English

IT CAN START WITH ME

Suitable for KS1

 Aims

To help children appreciate that by working together, big problems can be solved.

 Preparation and materials

- The assembly is based around a simple song sung to the tune of 'He's got the whole world in his hands' (many versions available, including no. 19 in the BBC songbook, *Come and Praise*).

 Assembly

1. Introduce and teach the song, singing it through a few times.

> It takes lots of people to change the world
> It takes lots of people to change the world
> It takes lots of people to change the world
> But it can start with me.
>
> If we work together, we can change the world
> If we work together, we can change the world
> If we work together, we can change the world
> And it can start with me.
>
> One small change can change the world
> Just one small change can change the world
> Yes one small change can change the world
> And it can start with me.

2. Ask the children what they would most like to change to make the world a better place for everyone. Value all ideas and pick one that seems theoretically possible, such as enough food for everyone or an end to a particular conflict that the children may have heard of.

   Pick a child whom you think can take a joke. Ask him or her to stand up. Say, 'Go and sort that out, please, Mahinda, and if you could be back by playtime that would be good. Now on to the next problem … '

   Ask the volunteer and the rest of the children why what you just asked was silly:

   • Because it's a big problem.
   • Because 'Mahinda' can't solve it on his own and he has to be at school.
   • It would cost a lot of money.

3. Ask, should we just give up, then, or can the words of our song help us to see the answer?
4. Explain that there are some very big problems around the world. Lots of people are hungry; others don't have clean water; many people are ill but could be cured by simple medicines; some people cannot afford to pay for food and shelter; and sometimes unexpected disasters happen. Here's just one story from a young girl called Sylvia:

Sylvia is a young girl who lives with her family in Sri Lanka, an island near India. Their house used to be beside the sea. But a few years ago, at Christmas time, a giant wave called a tsunami hit the island, and their home was completely washed away by the water. Huge waves carried Sylvia out to sea. She was separated from her family and all alone in the middle of the sea. She managed to cling to a log and held on to it for more than 24 hours. At last, an army helicopter spotted her and rescued her. Sadly, her nine-year-old brother and her best friend weren't so lucky; they both died.

Explain that the children might think that this is one of those impossible situations – how could anyone do anything to help? But now, some years later, things are better for Sylvia, and for thousands of other people who lost everything in the tsunami. Sylvia still misses her brother and her friend who died, but lots of people all over the world have shown that they care for Sylvia and the other victims of the tsunami by sending money and other kinds of help so that they can rebuild their homes and their lives.

5. Finish by saying that the world faces very big problems and no one can just pop out and sort them out as you asked 'Mahinda' to, but many people work hard every day to make the world a better place. And, like the song says, 'It can start with me'. Sing the song again.

 Time for reflection

It can start with me.
What can I do?
How can I help?
How can I make a difference?

It takes lots of people to change the world.
Can I be one of them?

If we work together, we can change the world.
Can I help to make things better?

One small change can change the world.
And it can start with me.

 Prayer

Dear God,
Thank you for all the good things that we have:
our food, our shelter, our families and friends, our school.

We think of people who don't have so many good things
and we thank you that there are people working to make a
fairer, better world.
Please help me to be part of that,
because if we work together, we can change the world.
Amen.

Class activities

1 Actions

Make up actions to accompany the song. Children could do this in groups, teaching their actions to the rest of the class.

Music, Dance

2 Posters

Ask the children to draw illustrated posters on the theme of 'Help Sylvia and her friends'. They will need to think about:

- What image (picture) to show on the poster.
- What colours to use to make it eye-catching.
- What words should be on the poster and how they should be written.

Art and design

3 Life in school

Talk about how 'It can start with me' can also be about life in school, about sharing and being helpful to other people. Ask for examples and then encourage the children to develop 'It can start with me' phrases such as:

- We need to be kinder and it can start with me.
- We need to listen to each other better and it can start with me.
- We need to save energy and recycle more and it can start with me.

Citizenship, PSHE

4 Lyrics

Turn the 'It can start with me' words into song lyrics for one of your favourite assembly songs. You could use the theme of 'Our school', with each verse celebrating a different aspect: children, staff, things we do, caring for each other, our school buildings.

English, Music

DEVELOPMENT, CHARITY, LOVE

Suitable for Whole School

Aims

To explore the meaning of the word 'development' as a process that helps people to help themselves.

Preparation and materials

- This assembly is linked to the KS1 assembly **Development – change for the better** (pages 2–6). This assembly can easily be adapted to become KS2 only or elements of each assembly can be combined.
- You'll need to be able to show the following, either on cards or using a board:

  Charity = Love
  Development

- Prepare four children to read the examples of development (pages 12–13).

Assembly

1. Ask what the children think the word 'charity' means. Value those responses that concern notions of giving money and help. Then point out that an old meaning of the word, and the one on which the modern meaning is based, is that charity equals 'love'. Write or display this as a formula: Charity = Love.
2. Say that you don't mean romantic love or Valentine's Day, but something that fits this description. Read a version of St Paul's famous words from the New Testament in 1 Corinthians 13, or use this paraphrase:

11

I might talk the talk but without love – forget it!
I might be super faithful and super clever but without love
– forget it!
I might tell everyone how generous I am but without love
– forget it!

Love is patient and kind, puts up with a lot.
It's not big-headed or rude or not
thinking 'I'm number one, I'm the best'.
It puts others first; love is the greatest.

3. Display the word Development, and ask the children what they think it means. If there are KS1 children present who have experienced the **Development – change for the better** assembly ask them in particular.

Work round to the idea that development means a change for the better, and that this is what love means too: changing ourselves to put other people first and helping their lives to change for the better. But we often think that 'charity' means just giving money, and some say that money sent to help people in poorer countries doesn't really make a difference.

Ask the children to think about these examples of development, read by the four prepared children.

Reader 1: In the Philippines a local organization gave farmers worms to help them make fertilizer which helped them grow better crops. So they made more money, and so they could make things better for themselves.

Readers: Development, charity, love.

Reader 2: In Ghana a local organization gave farmers edible snails to grow. When baby snails were produced the farmers gave some of them to the organization to give to other farmers. So they made things better for themselves and for other people.

Readers: Development, charity, love.

Reader 3: In India a local organization has trained children to show other people when their drinking water is safe to drink, so that they don't get ill. The organization set it up and the children have carried on the work – they make things better for themselves.

Readers: Development, charity, love.
Reader 4: In Cambodia, local people have been trained to find landmines. Making life safer – making things better for themselves.
Readers: Development, charity, love.
Reader 1: All around the world, charities and local organizations are helping people.
Reader 2: But they don't just give them things and then forget them.
Reader 3: They get them started so that there can be development.
Reader 4: That's change for the better.
Reader 1: Making things better for themselves.
Readers: Development, charity, love.

 ## Time for reflection

Development, charity, love.
What do these words mean to you?
What do they mean for the world?
What could they mean for you today?

 ## Prayer

Dear God,
We thank you that we can all be involved in development – helping people to make things better for themselves.
Thank you that you have made a world in which people can work together and help each other.
Please help us to show charity, another word for love, to other people.
Amen.

 ## Class activities

1 Definitions
Talk again about the words development, charity, and love. Can the children come up with their own definitions?

English

2 Love

Look at St Paul's words about love in 1 Corinthians 13 in a modern translation of the Bible, and then at the paraphrase used in the assembly. Choose one phrase from either and use it as the basis for a story, perhaps about someone who talks a lot but doesn't listen, or about someone who has the opportunity to be big-headed or rude but resists the temptation.

English

3 Choral or rap

Create a choral or rap presentation based on the 'Love' paraphrase used in the assembly. Can the children write a chorus that everyone can join in with while individuals speak or rap the other lines?

English, Music

4 Posters

Using any version of 1 Corinthians 13, or your own paraphrase, create an illustrated poster.

English, Art and design

5 Group research

Research examples of development that clearly show change for the better and people helping themselves. You could start by looking at the websites of development charities. Working in groups, children could present their findings to the rest of the class or in an assembly.

Research, Presentation skills

KYLIE'S DREAM

Suitable for Whole School

 Aims

To acknowledge that some children feel overpowered by the world's problems and to provide an imaginative way of countering this through the message that we can all take action to make a positive difference.

 Preparation and materials

- This assembly is based around a story which takes about five minutes to read, so you may prefer to use the story in class prior to the assembly, or to split it in two, spreading it across two assemblies.

 Assembly

1. Read, or briefly recall by question and answer, the story 'Kylie's dream', below.

Kylie's dream*
Some people love football and some people can't stand it, and other people ... well, they're neither here nor there. Ask them if they like football and they might say, 'S'all right' or 'Yeah, I like it okay'; but if you asked Kylie about football you'd be stuck there for half a day while she rabbited on. Because Kylie didn't just love football, she lived football. Her dad said that if you looked inside her head you wouldn't see a brain, just a tiny football pitch with miniature people running around and a tinsy little ball flying all over the place. Kylie thought that her dad was mad, and just jealous because he, in a million, zillion years couldn't play as well as she could. Kylie was captain of her school team, Landsdown Road Primary, and tonight they would be playing in a crucial

15

cup-tie match against Willingborough. *They* would, but not Kylie.

'Oh Mum, please, please let me go to school this afternoon, pleeeease,' whined Kylie from the sofa, but her mum just shook her head. One look at Kylie, team captain, would tell you that today she was more like Kylie, team mascot – if your mascot was a sort of droopy wet rag with a streaming nose and eyes and a temperature hot enough to fry an egg.

Kylie was poorly. She'd been off school all morning and had hoped she would be better by this afternoon, but now she knew she would have to miss the match and that was all there was to it.

Inside, Kylie knew her mum was right. She did feel dreadful, and even if she made it to the pitch she'd be no use once she got there: one kick of the ball and she'd probably fall over; one header and she'd be knocked out. She knew all this, but knowing it didn't make things any better as she lay on the sofa watching daytime TV.

She was hardly aware of what was going on – what had she just watched? Antique home decorating at a cookery auction, or something? Then she realized the News was starting and Kylie tried to pay attention.

'Now an update on the drought situation in … ' the newsreader began, but Kylie had started to doze again. She drifted off into a sleepy world but the News sort of drifted in too. She heard the newsreader say, 'It is estimated that 10,000 have lost their lives in the conflict in … ' And later she heard, 'Doctors are losing hope in their battle against … ' But mostly it was just a blur, a blurry mix-up of words – famine, drought, disease, illness, war. 'Why does the News have to be so miserable?' thought Kylie as she slipped into a dream.

In her dream, Kylie was still lying on the sofa, still watching the News, but now the News was different. The newsreader was saying, 'News just in: unexpected rainfall in the drought area brings hope to millions; peace has finally broken out in the long-standing war; and three exciting new medical breakthroughs have just been announced.'

'Oh, that's better,' said Kylie, sitting up and paying

attention as the newsreader went on: 'Now sport. Tonight sees the crucial cup-tie match between Landsdown Road Primary and Willingborough. Landsdown are playing without their ace player and captain Kylie Barnes which is a great shame because … '

In her dream Kylie knew that the newsreader's next words were going to be bad and sure enough, as night follows day, out they came.

' … which is a great shame because the prime minister has just announced that every one of those good things depends on Kylie Barnes scoring tonight. If she scores one goal, the drought ends; if she scores two, the war ends as well; if she scores three, then the medical breakthroughs happen too. Each goal scored is another goal reached in the search for a perfect world. What a shame she won't be playing tonight.'

Before you could say 'It's only a dream', Kylie was up and out of the house. She had to get to school and play in the match. Now it was more important than anything; now it was *the* most important thing.

It was chucking it down with rain as Kylie battled her way through the streets to school. She was battling the horrid wet, windy weather – her clothes were soaked through; she was battling her own body – she felt so awful that she just wanted to go to sleep right there in the muddy wet gutter; and she was battling her fear that she'd be too late, that she wouldn't score enough goals and that she wouldn't help create a perfect world.

She passed a shop window where rows of TVs were showing a war, a drought, hungry people – all the bad things in the world, going over them again and again. It was horrible. Kylie tried to rush past the shop but she couldn't seem to get away; the window and its TVs seemed to go on for ever and ever.

Then, suddenly she was there, at school, at the match, in her kit, and she was running on to the pitch and she felt great.

Maggs passed to Cockle, Davis to Patel and Patel to Kylie Barnes, a beautiful pass. Excellent control by Kylie Barnes, this girl is magic. She passes one defender, she dodges two, she swerves past three with the grace and skill of a football-playing gazelle and she shoots: she scores.

Landsdown take the lead and that's an end to drought. Now what can this girl do about the war? She has the ball, will she pass? No, she sees an opening and she scores! A magnificent goal from the Landsdown lass. Now, can she make it three and kick disease out of play? The ball's coming her way again, and oh, it's a bit high, she jumps, she heads it, but no – it's too high for her and she falls to the ground.

She's out, she's out cold.

Everything went black in Kylie's dream. 'I need to score, I need to score,' she kept saying over and over again.

Kylie woke up; her mum had switched off the TV. 'Mum, Mum, I need to score. I've got to,' mumbled Kylie.

Her mum sat down next to her on the sofa. 'Someone's been having a dream,' she said, 'or a nightmare.'

'A dream ... it was, I think it was ... it was a dream, wasn't it?' said Kylie in a confused way.

Her mum gave her a drink of water and then listened while Kylie told her all about the strange dream. 'And Mum, I feel so bad; there're so many bad things going on in the world and I can't do anything about them.'

Her mum took a deep breath. 'First of all,' she said, 'just because the News has three bad things on in a row doesn't mean that everything's terrible, does it? I mean, they don't put on all the work that is being done around the world to help people find solutions to the problems they face. All those bad things are real, Kylie, but you have to remember that they're not the whole picture. Lots of good things are happening all the time but you don't see them on the News. I bet if you tried you could think of a hundred good things that have happened this month.'

'But that doesn't stop the bad things happening, does it?' said Kylie. 'I mean the bad things are still there, aren't they?'

'Well, yes,' her mum went on, 'but in your dream you thought that everything depended on you, but life's not like that. You can't put everything right all by yourself, but you could do something to make a difference. We can all do something.'

'What sort of things?' asked Kylie, who was starting to feel better now.

'You could give some of your pocket money to a charity. You could join a sponsored event. You could ... '

But Kylie interrupted her. 'No, Mum, I could *run* a sponsored event – do you know what it would be?'

'Would it involve football, by any chance?' asked her mum – but I think we all know the answer to that one, don't we?

2. Story questions: What were the things that made Kylie sad and anxious (stressed)? Why do you think she felt like that? What did her mum say to her when Kylie woke up? What do you think Kylie will do to raise money?

3. What examples can the children give of ways of raising money to help other people? Try to get a range including collections and sponsorship but also fun events. Stress that fund-raising can be an 'everyone's a winner' situation, as the people raising money often do enjoyable things together (sponsored games or fêtes, for example) and sometimes get extra fit as well (sponsored runs and swims). Run through these real-life crazy fund-raising ideas:

   • The staff of a primary school sponsored the headteacher to go to the post office to pay in school donations – in her pyjamas!
   • A ladies darts team did a walkabout around their town one Friday evening in fancy dress. They followed this with a 12-hour darts marathon.
   • Quite a few people have had their heads shaved to raise money through sponsorship.
   • Two middle-school pupils asked to do maths all day and were sponsored for it.
   • A pub ran an oatcake-eating competition.
   • A day nursery had a wacky hair day and face painting – including all staff!
   • Harold the Horse and Emma the Emu held a sponsored wacky walk – in panto horse and emu costumes!
   • A company ran a 'gunge-off', where customers, suppliers and staff paid to vote for which boss got gunged.

- A girl who said 'I never shut up' went for a whole day without speaking (sponsored silence).

Time for reflection

Kylie loved football and planned to use her talent to raise funds for people less fortunate than her. Other people have held sponsored silences, run in fancy dress – even done maths all day! What could you do to raise funds to make a difference – and perhaps have some fun at the same time!

Prayer

Dear God,
Thank you that we all have talents and gifts –
things that we do well and things that we love doing.
Please help us to use our talents to help other people
    whenever we can.
Amen.

Class activities

1 Kylie's dream – special edition!
Using the words of 'Kylie's dream', create a book. Cut up a copy of the words and draw some illustrations. Paste words and illustrations into a book format. Design the cover and write the back cover copy – a few words about the book that will entice people to buy it.

English, Art and design

2 Kylie's dream – the sequel!
Write a story about what happens next. Does Kylie put her plan into action? Does it all go smoothly or are there problems along the way? Perhaps she has another dream?

English

3 Research
Find out about as many different types of fund-raising as you can. The *BBC Children in Need* website has some ideas to get you started. What is the craziest idea you can find? Which forms of fund-raising are most popular? You could conduct a survey of your class or school to find out. Can you show these results as a graph or a pie chart?

Research, Maths

4 My dream
Write a speech called 'My dream', telling people what you'd most like to happen in the world. A speech is written to be read out loud, so you'll need to think about:

- Short sentences, so you don't run out of breath!
- Words that are easy to say without 'tripping up'.
- A clear structure: introduction, developing your idea, summary.
- Something that will be interesting to listen to.
- Most important – practise out loud!

English

5 Maths
How much money would be raised in a sponsored swim if 40 people were sponsored at 5p per length and:

- 1 person swam 50 lengths
- 10 people swam 40 lengths
- 15 people swam 30 lengths
- 10 people swam 20 lengths
- 4 people swam 10 lengths?

(Answer: 1,140 lengths × 5p = £57)

Maths

FREEDOM

Suitable for KS2

 ### Aims

To explore the idea of freedom in relation to slavery and poverty.

 ### Preparation and materials

- A key element of this assembly is a dance to be prepared in advance by a class of children. The assembly will work without this element but will have much greater impact if a dance is included. Suggestions for the dance are given below.
- For the interview you will need five children (children 1–4 and Pyram) and an interviewer (which could be you).

Dance outline

The theme of the dance is slavery and freedom. The simple pattern allows for four sections: enslavement, life as a slave, rebellion, freedom.

Music

Any powerful music with strong rhythmic elements can be used. Not too long – two to three minutes is probably about right, depending on the time available to devise and rehearse. The following are suggestions:

- an extract from *Night on a Bare Mountain* (Mussorgsky)
- an extract from 'Mars' from the *Planets Suite* (Holst)
- 'The Immigrant Song' (Led Zeppelin)
- even the *Dr Who* theme tune (Ron Grainer).

Suggested movement motifs

- *Enslavement*: a small number of 'catchers' move stealthily while their 'prey' go about their daily activities, for example,

22

planting crops, or playing. The catchers slowly encircle the prey and then pounce using their outstretched arms to form a cage. The prey cannot escape, though they try pushing against the cage – it holds firm until gradually the new slaves sink down through hunger and tiredness.

- *Life as a slave*: use repetitive exhausting work movements for the slaves and casual sauntering but powerful movements for the slave masters. The movements of the masters are unpredictable as they lash out or simply point; the slaves react, perhaps using slow motion to show falling to the ground or recoiling in fear.
- *Rebellion*: the slave masters settle down to sleep and the slaves huddle together in the centre of the space. They look exhausted – but then on a signal (music cue?) they find new strength and leap out into the space and several of them surround each sleeping master.
- *Freedom*: actions to suggest throwing off of chains, throwing away tools. A final tableau includes the pose from the Statue of the Unknown Slave in Port-au-Prince, Haiti's capital city: crouching with fist raised in the air, representing freedom and victory over slavery.

 Assembly

1. Explain that in today's assembly we're going to find out about a country called Haiti. The name Haiti means 'land of mountains'. It is a very beautiful country that is warm all year round.

   Haiti was ruled by France from 1697 until 1804. The French brought thousands of slaves from Africa in ships to Haiti to work on the sugar cane plantations. Let's find out what it was like to be a slave. Introduce the interview.

   Interviewer: How do you spend your days?
   Child 1:   I work so hard all day, every day. I have to cut sugar cane for my masters. If I don't work hard enough, they beat me.
   Interviewer: But do you get paid well for your work?

Child 2:   No! I don't get paid at all! My master owns me, so I have to do what he says. He sells the sugar cane we cut, so he makes lots of money.

Interviewer: Your masters brought you here from Africa. What do you think of your new home?

Child 3:   Well, I've only seen this sugar plantation. I can't go anywhere or do anything except work here. I didn't ask to come here. I was forced to.

Interviewer: That's terrible. What are your hopes for the future?

Child 4:   I just want to be free. I want to be able to work for myself. I want to have my own house and family. I want to live my own life.

Thank the children for taking part and ask them to sit down.

2. Most slaves felt the same way, and many rebelled against their masters. In 1804, after many years of fighting, Haitians won their freedom from their French rulers. The French left and the people of Haiti ruled themselves again. But although there are no slaves in Haiti any more, and even after 200 years of freedom, life is still very hard for the people there. Let's hear from Pyram, who lives in Haiti. He is part of a dance troupe. They go into schools and perform a special dance celebrating 200 years of freedom. The dance tells the history of Haiti.

Interviewer: Pyram, what is life like for people in Haiti now?

Pyram: Many people are very poor. There aren't many jobs around.

Interviewer: How do the people celebrate 200 years of freedom?

Pyram: Well, we love to celebrate, to dance and make music. But our country is not really free.

Interviewer: Why not? Your people aren't slaves any more, are they?

Pyram: No, we are not slaves, but my country is very poor. We need freedom from poverty, so that every child has enough to eat, can go to school and can feel safe and secure.

Interviewer: What are you doing about it?

Pyram: Our children are our hope for the future. They need to be strong leaders one day. Our dance will help children understand their history, so they can move into the future.

3. Introduce the class's version of Pyram's dance.

Time for reflection

Ask the children to think about the dance that they have just seen. What does it say to them? You could ask them to think quietly about this and then perhaps share some of their thoughts with the rest of the assembly.

Prayer

Dear God,
We pray for the people of Haiti,
that as they remember their freedom from slavery
they will be able to work towards freedom from poverty.
Thank you for the freedom that we enjoy.
Amen.

Class activities

1 National flags

Talk about where the children come from. Which countries are represented within the class? You could talk about where their parents, grandparents and ancestors come from. Then ask children to look up the flags of the countries mentioned (using <www.flagspot.net>). Discuss what the symbols represent on these flags. Ask the children to draw a flag of their own, to represent their background and what is important to them. What colours will they use and what simple, clear images?

Citizenship, Art and design

2 Haiti's flag

Show the children where Haiti is on a map or globe and explain some of its history, based on web research. Use <www.flagspot.net> to look at the Haitian and French flags. The Haitian flag uses the same colours as the French flag, but with no white – this was to show that the white leaders had left. The stripes of the Haitian flag are turned on their side compared to those of the French flag, to show that the country has moved away from its slave past when black people had no rights.

Discuss together what the children think of the Haitian flag – did the Haitian people make a good choice when they picked this design?

PSHE, Citizenship

3 Rights of the child

What are rights? Can the children think of any rights that they have? Make a list of rights on the board and discuss which the children think are most important and why. Ask the children what they think it might be like to have no rights.

Explain that every child in the world has rights. The United Nations has written a list of children's rights called the UN Convention on the Rights of the Child (UNCRC). Use the 'Children have rights!' worksheet (page 27) to show them some of their rights.

PSHE, Citizenship

4 *Restaveks*

Explain to your class about *restaveks* – children who have been given away by their parents to work as domestic servants. Ask them to imagine what life would be like as a *restavek* child in Haiti. How would it be different from their own life? Then ask them to read each right on their worksheet, decide whether they enjoy that right, and give an example. Ask them to think about whether *restavek* children in Haiti have each right, giving examples of whether they do or don't in the right-hand column.

Citizenship, PSHE

Children have rights!

Here are just some of the rights that you are entitled to.

	Me	A *restavek* child in Haiti
You have the right to enough to eat, adequate clothes and a roof over your head.		
No one has the right to hurt you. Adults must protect you from violence and abuse.		
You have the right to education, and for primary education to be free.		
You have the right not to do harmful work and you can't work when you are very young.		
You have the right to live with your parents and keep in touch with both of them if they separate. If you haven't got a family, you have the right to special care.		

Views from other faiths
on freedom

We belong to one big human family, which includes all of humankind on this planet.

H H the Dalai Lama, Buddhist

Call no one high or low. God, the one potter has made all alike. God's light alone pervades all creation.

Guru Nanak, Sikh

He has sent me to bring good news to the poor, to proclaim liberty to the captives and to set free the oppressed.

Luke 4.18–19, Christian

Freedom is never voluntarily given by the oppressors, it must be demanded by the oppressed.

Martin Luther King, Christian

You shall love your neighbour as yourself.

Mark 12.31, Christian

If anyone walks with an oppressor to strengthen him, knowing that he is an oppressor, he has gone forth from Islam.

Hadith, Islam

You can't separate peace from freedom because no one can be at peace unless he has his freedom.

Malcolm X, Muslim

No society can possibly be built on a denial of individual freedom.

Mahatma Gandhi, Hindu

5   Views from other faiths

Ask the children to look at the 'Views from other faiths' worksheet (page 28). Can they pick one of these and create an illustrated version of it to form part of a wall display? Can they say why they have picked this particular statement?

RE, Art and design

CHRISTMAS: GIFTS, GIVING GOATS AND GRATITUDE

Suitable for Whole School

 Aims

To think about gifts and giving, and about the needs of people around the world at Christmas time.

 Preparation and materials

- You will need an accomplice who is prepared to hide during the start of the assembly and make goat noises to interrupt you! This could be another member of staff or a child.
- Optional: Find out this year's prices (from development charity websites) for giving goats, and other gifts such as training, schooling, etc.
- Optional: Flipchart/whiteboard for recording children's ideas.

 Assembly

1. Begin the assembly in a solemn mode. Perhaps you could play serious music as the children enter. Say that you want to talk very seriously about the serious side of Christmas today, so let's all be serious for a few moments of seriously serious thought. Leave pauses as you speak and then a big pause at the end. Open your mouth as if about to continue …

Goat noise

Look slightly embarrassed and then decide to ignore the interruption. Ask the children what they believe will be the best-selling Christmas gift this year. Take all their suggestions, and in addition to the top toy of the year be sure to mention things like MP3s, jewellery, perfume, DVDs, etc. To add to the 'serious' mood you could list the ideas on a flipchart or whiteboard.

2. Once the suggestions are in, return to your solemn mood, with some tutting in disapproval at the list of gifts. Say something like, 'It makes you think, doesn't it … I don't know … '

Goat noise

Look askance and then attempt to continue: 'As I was saying … '

Goat noise

You begin to lose it at this point, saying that you've had enough of being interrupted while you try to deal with this serious Christmas business in a serious fashion.

Goat noise

Angry now, you go round the assembly space seeking out the source of the noise. Eventually find the hiding place and pull your accomplice out by the arm or ear (agree this first!).

Ask the accomplice what on earth they think they're doing, interrupting your important and serious assembly.

The accomplice then explains that they were simply trying to remind you that goats are one of the top Christmas gifts, alongside bees, chickens and cows. You could include some banter at this point about it sounding more like a strangled ferret or similar, to establish the idea that the sound was meant to be a goat.

3. Now show your interest in what your accomplice is saying. Ask questions, eliciting these main facts.

People give money to charities to buy a gift for a friend. The charity then uses this money to support local organizations in poorer parts of the world. These organizations buy animals or other items for people in poorer parts of the world, helping them to become self-sufficient (look after themselves). The friend gets a card saying what their gift is and what part of the world it is going to.

The animal gifts can then be shared. For example, two goats might breed to produce more goats which can then go to more families. Then they breed to make more goats and on it goes. Each goat produces milk and can be used for food.

Sometimes money is given to local organizations that run projects such as sending a child to school, or perhaps computer training so that people can get jobs.

You could give a few examples of this year's gifts and prices.

4. Say, almost despite yourself, that sponsoring organizations on the other side of the world to give goats and chickens to local people sounds fun! Your accomplice points out that it *is* a fun way to give a gift, and it can greatly help people around the world.

 ## Time for reflection

What do I most want for Christmas?
Special gifts: games, toys, music players, clothes, vouchers?
Special times: family meals, parties, fun and games, time off school, playing with my friends?
Special hopes: peace around the world, an end to war, food for the hungry, shelter for the homeless?
Special ideas: goats as gifts, bees as surprises … a gift of love sent around the world!

 ## Prayer

Dear God,
Thank you for this special time of year.
We think of those who don't have enough to eat or don't have healthcare or shelter.
Thank you that there is enough for everyone in this world.
Please help us to do what we can to share the world's resources.
And thank you for brilliant gift ideas like cows and goats and even giant snails!
Amen.

Class activities

1 What do you do?

Give each child an outline of a Christmas tree and ask them to write or draw in it things that they think of when they hear the word 'Christmas'. Discuss what kinds of things people in the class do on Christmas Day, whether they celebrate it or not.

PSHE, RE

2 Christmas lists

If they receive presents at Christmas or at other times, ask the children what they are hoping to get this year. Is there a common 'most wished for' item? Have they ever received a funny or useless present? What was it? Use this to recap the charity presents in the assembly.

English, PSHE

3 Charity Christmas gifts

Use the internet and catalogues brought in from home to create a database of charity Christmas gifts. Divide them into categories such as gifts made abroad, fair trade items, live animal gifts, gifts given to people in other countries. Several items will be in more than one category so how will you organize your database?

IT, Research skills

4 Wishes for this Christmas

Divide the class into pairs and ask them to talk about what they would wish for children around the world this Christmas. It could be for children generally or for children from a specific country that they may have heard about on the News. Pairs should feed back to the rest of the class. The various wishes could be written on decorated stars to hang from a class Christmas tree or to make a display.

PSHE, Art and design

IT'S ALL IN THE MIX!

Suitable for Whole School

 ### Aims

To explore the idea of working together, partnerships across the world including UK charities, and that everyone has a part to play.

 ### Preparation and materials

- You will need the ingredients to make a tasty ice cream sundae: ice cream, chopped banana, chocolate sauce, broken biscuit, tinned cherries, squirty cream, etc.
- A blender and one cup of milk to make a milkshake.
- Optional: Ice cream cones, bowls and spoons.
- Old food boxes/packets with new labels stuck on: 'Charity', 'Local partners', 'Seeds', 'Sheep'.
- Five paper plates or circles showing: a school sign; a hospital sign; picture of bread; large X; smiley face.
- Volunteers to hold up and explain the paper plates.

 ### Assembly

1. Introduce your ingredients and show how you can make a delicious ice cream sundae from them. Take your time, talking about what you're doing in a TV chef style: 'A quality, tasty ice cream base'; 'Squirty cream – and an extra squirt for good luck'; 'One of my favourite dessert ingredients – tinned cherries, yum'; 'and to finish off, sugar sprinkles: terrible food value, great fun and just look at those vibrant colours'.
2. When you've made your sundae, invite a couple of children to try it and ask for their comments. Ham it up if you want, showing exaggerated concern at the slightest criticism and gushing enthusiasm for any praise!

3. Explain that these are the perfect ingredients for an ice cream sundae – but the same ingredients could be used to make a milkshake, just by adding a cup of milk. Go through the same procedure, making an ice cream-based milk shake: one cup of milk and two scoops of ice cream; add other ingredients to taste such as cherries, and perhaps some squirty cream and/or sprinkles on top. Again, do your TV chef impression and invite some tasters to try the result.

4. Suggest another possibility – the ice cream sundae could be served in an ice cream cone. Create this as above, if you have time. Then suggest a fourth dessert using the same ingredients, but serve the ice cream separately: tinned cherries sprinkled with nuts, with ice cream on the side. Again, make this if you have time.

5. Stress that you have been putting more or less the same ingredients into each dessert, but mixing them differently to create different outcomes – or puddings, as scientists call them!

6. Explain that you're now going to talk about different sorts of ingredients that make different sorts of outcomes. This is called *mejores días*, which means 'better days' in Bolivia. It's a recipe that is very important for the people there who are being moved off their farmland by cattle ranchers. The same recipe works for people all over the world.

   The first ingredient can come from right here. Hold up the 'Charity' box. This box could feature a flier or some other indication of a recent fund-raising event (such as Christian Aid Week), with which the children will feel familiar.

   Next add 'local organizations'. These local organizations work with local people in the rainforest to protect their land from ranchers, and look after crops and animals. Show the box. This ingredient helps people understand that they have the right to own and protect their land.

   That means we can sow seeds, and we've got bananas, mangoes, cocoa and trees. Show 'Seeds' box.

   Now we can add some animals for variety; it could be sheep or chickens. One local partner in Bolivia has an interesting way of providing sheep. One group of families receives 20 sheep – 1 male and 19 females – and that number soon multiplies! Once a community has 100 sheep, they pass on 20 to another community. Of course, families in the community can sell the crops and animals that they don't need for themselves. Show 'Sheep' box.

Our recipe for *mejores días* is now complete. By adding all these things together the people can improve their lives, by having enough food to eat, and some money to spare, as our volunteers will show you. Ask your volunteers to hold up the plates and explain what they mean for the people of Bolivia.

- *School*: children attend primary school in their village, then families can afford to send them away to secondary school.
- *Hospital*: people can afford to visit a clinic or buy medicine if someone in their family is ill.
- *Bread*: communities can afford to buy bread and other foodstuffs that they cannot grow.
- *X*: people can vote in elections to have a say on local issues.
- *Smiley face*: people no longer live in fear of ranchers taking their land and can plan for a better future.

7. Say that one way of remembering how this works is to think of the phrase: 'You add, we multiply'. You add the ingredients, and the people who receive them work with them to create something more.

 ## Time for reflection

Let's be quiet for a moment and remember that we can all bring *mejores días* or better days to friends, family, school, local community and world community. If everyone adds one small thing, it will soon multiply.

From seeds to trees (*fingers move upwards*)
From earth to sky (*circle-point upwards*)
You add, we multiply (*fingers make + and x sign*).

For food to eat,
New food to try (*mime eating*)
You add, we multiply.
For crops to sell
Then goods to buy (*hands give, hands take*)
You add, we multiply.

For a safe and healthy life (*smiley face and thumbs up*)
You add, we multiply.

Prayer

The world is made for working together.
Like a delicious dessert it needs ingredients
and human minds to dream up the mix,
and human hands to mix it up
to make something good to share.
Thank you, God, that ours is a world of sharing.
Help us all to learn to share.
Amen.

Class activities

1 Where we live

Talk to the class about the area they live in. What is it like?
Are there houses and shops or is it rural? Ask them to draw a
map of their local area, including their house, school and
other places they regularly visit. Talk together about how the
community works, and how some facilities, such as schools,
medical centres, playgrounds, shops and so on, have to be
shared by everyone.

English, Geography, PSHE

2 Comparing lives

Read Sara's story.

Sara Amblo Rosel lives with her parents in a village in a
rainforest in Bolivia, which is the poorest country in South
America. Sara starts her day with a breakfast of bread and a
hot drink. She heads off early for school so that she can get a
seat, because there aren't enough chairs to go round! School
finishes at lunchtime, and after a game of football Sara starts
her chores. She cleans the house, then washes clothes, pots
and pans in the river. Then she waters her family's crops,
hunts for eggs among the hens, and checks their woolless
sheep. Some days she rows down the river to work on the
family *chaco* (plot of land).

She says: 'My *chaco* is beautiful, with cocoa, banana, papaya, mandarin and mango trees. There are birds that copy what you say, and monkeys play in the trees.' But things haven't always been so good. Life became difficult when cattle ranchers tried to take their land and clear the forest to make room for their animals. The Centre for Research and Training of Peasant Farmers (CIPCA), an organization that is supported by charities in the UK and Ireland, has helped Sara and her family. CIPCA has provided training and education to help rainforest communities. It trains them how to produce different crops and meat so they have a better diet and a source of income. CIPCA also provides seeds and animals, basic tools and equipment.

Sara is only eight years old, but she understands what a difference CIPCA has made to her community. She says, 'We have lots of different things to eat. Before I only ate rice, now I eat all the things we grow.'

Because of the money her family makes from their crops, Sara knows that her father will be able to pay for her and her older brother to go away to secondary school. Sara wants to be a teacher when she grows up. She knows that she and her community will have *mejores días* – better days – with the help of CIPCA.

Split the class into small groups and ask them to think up three questions they would like to ask Sara about her life, and three things they would tell her about their lives. Discuss similarities and differences between the children's life and Sara's life.

PSHE, Geography, English

3   Here and there mapping
Sara's community is made up of 22 families who live in houses in a circle round a playing field. The houses are built of wood with wicker roofs. In the circle there is also a chapel, a meeting hall and a brick-built school. Water comes from the nearby river. From this information and that provided in Sara's story, children can make a map of her village.

Look back at the maps of their community and ask them to discuss the advantages or disadvantages of living in each place. Would the children be allowed to go off with the sheep and row down the river, as Sara is? Why, or why not?

Geography

4 Bolivian background

Ask the children what they know about South America and Bolivia. Split the class into groups and using maps, atlases, the internet and other available resources challenge each group to make up either a factsheet, a ten-question quiz, or a podcast about Bolivia.

Geography, English, IT

FOOTBALL MAD – MAD FOOTBALL!

Suitable for Whole School

 Aims

To use the idea of rules in a sporting event to explore how we all need to agree and live by rules in our communities.

 Preparation and materials

- The first part of the assembly is a mock TV sports programme, so some opening music would be good, such as the theme music of *Match of the Day* or 'Beautiful Day' by U2.
- Some simple props such as microphone and clipboard could be used, and you could dress in an appropriate style.
- Some children could be rehearsed to read Jessica's story.

 Assembly

1. Begin with the mock TV sports programme. Play the theme music, then launch into presenter mode.

   Good evening, I'm Gary Vinegar, and welcome back to this special World Cup Final edition of *Match of the Night*. If you've just tuned in, it's half-time and what a first half you've missed: so far, England are leading Brazil 23 goals to 22.
      Oh, I ought to explain – just a few minutes before the match, an announcement was made by someone official who felt that the other World Cup matches have been a bit boring, a bit 'samey'. So for the final match they've changed the rules. In fact, they've got rid of them altogether. Players can now do whatever they want.

Wayne Spooney soon got into the swing of this and was quick to combine his trademark crossing with some lovely netball passes. About 20 minutes in, Ronald Chino hid the ball in his hair, shouted, 'Look over there!' and ran right the way up the pitch to throw the ball into the goal.

But the biggest stroke of genius had to be when the England manager sent on the World Cup mascot – a two-metre-tall lion. Unfortunately this caused a bit of a fight between the England and Brazilian coaches. But as there are no rules, the managers can do what they like!

Let's return now to our commentators for the second half and see what ... Oh, the players have started already and aren't waiting for the whistle! In fact, they're just running out of the tunnel towards the goal and every player has a football in his hands. Oh, and here come the wives and girlfriends too – and they're all carrying footballs too. Er, quickly, over to John in the commentary box.

Play a bit of the music again and then fade it out.

2. Talk briefly about football and the fact that many people are 'football mad'; but if you don't have rules, you get mad football! Remind everyone that Brazil is one of the top teams in the world. Then introduce this story from Brazil.

Jessica's story

Football is played all over the world, but the rules of the game are the same wherever you are – and they're all important for the game to work.

In Brazil, there's a group of young people who also think rules are important – and not just for football. Passage House is a special refuge run by a local organization which helps young girls who have a difficult life at home or who live on the streets. The girls are looked after, receive medical care from doctors and dentists, and take part in classes, such as dance and drama, where they can talk about their problems.

Passage House gives young girls the opportunity to turn their lives around. But, in return, there are rules to follow. These include going to school, no fighting, and respecting each other. If they don't stick to the rules, they have to leave Passage House. It's like being given a red card.

Sixteen-year-old Jessica Lins Silva used to hang around on the streets and get into fights. But since spending time at Passage House, she says, 'I've learnt all sorts of things – how to behave properly, how to talk properly, how to think and analyse things. Before, if someone criticized me, I'd just want to hit them. Now I've learnt acceptable behaviour. I've changed.'

3. Point out that before she went to Passage House Jessica's life had very few rules, which meant she found herself in some dangerous situations. And whether it's at Passage House, on the football pitch, or at your school, rules exist so that we know what we can and cannot do, so we know how to act, and so that we stay safe.
4. Ask the children what they think would happen if there were no rules, like in the football match described above. Can they think of examples of when rules have been broken, either in their experience or something they've seen on TV or in a sports game? What happened?

 Time for reflection

Ask the children to think of a rule in sport, at home or at school that they have trouble keeping. What happens when this rule is broken?
Are all rules fair?
What should we do if we think a rule is unfair?

 Prayer

Dear God,
We thank you for the work at places like Passage House
and the rules they have to keep people safe.
Help us to keep the rules that keep us safe,
whether in sport, at home or at school,
and give us wisdom to know how to challenge rules that
    don't seem fair.
Amen.

Class activities

1 Football frenzy

Talk to the class about football. Who likes football? Who doesn't? Why? Who do they think will win the FA Cup/World Cup/other current tournament? Split the class into small groups and give each group a list of football rules – some real ones, some made up. Ask the group to sort out which are real rules and which aren't. Go through the answers and discuss why rules are important in football. This could be repeated with school rules and also applied to any other sport.

You can find the laws of football at the Football Association website <www.thefa.com>.

PE, PSHE

2 Keeping the rules

Talk about other situations where there are rules that children should obey, in school or at home. What do they think of the rules? Are all the rules fair? Is it ever OK to break rules? Explain that although rules are sometimes annoying, they are mostly there for the greater good.

Citizenship, PSHE

3 Leaflet making

Ask the children to imagine that they have just arrived at Passage House. How would they feel? What would they want to know? Ask half the class to design a welcome leaflet for people new to Passage House and the other half of the class to design one for new children at your school. Compare the finished leaflets and display them.

Art and design, Citizenship, PSHE

4 Stories

Write a story called 'The Day the Rules Changed'. It can be about any aspect of life in which there are rules, such as a sporting event, life in school; or bigger rule changes, such as children being allowed to do what adults can (for example, drive a car, teach in school), and adults having to behave as children (for example, set bedtimes, go to school).

English

5 Then and now
Create a class display showing different aspects of Jessica's life before and after living at Passage House.

Art and design

FLOWING MILK

Suitable for Whole School

Aims

To introduce the notion of fair trade and of working together in an organized fashion.

Preparation and materials

- You will need two jigsaw puzzles of at least 30 pieces each. They do not need to be identical but should be of roughly equal levels of difficulty. Charity shops are a good source of second-hand puzzles.
- Complete and stick down one puzzle in advance except for one single piece, so that you can easily and with a flourish complete it in the assembly. You will need to keep the puzzle hidden, so if the completed puzzle will fit in its box, so much the better. The other puzzle remains in its box in pieces.
- Two tables to do the puzzles on.

Assembly

1. Ask who likes jigsaw puzzles. Assemble a team of three or four children for a 'jigsaw challenge'. Say that you will compete against the team to be the first to finish – and you'll even give them a head start.

   Set the team to work making up the puzzle on a table at the front. Then, after a while and with a big flourish, pick up your own jigsaw box and show your puzzle. Make a big show of slotting the last piece into place and call a halt to the competition.

2. Talk about the game and why it wasn't fair. In your explanation, use the word 'organized': something like, 'Well, you can't blame me for being organized in advance, can you?' Stress the point that your opponents didn't stand a chance;

45

they couldn't compete with someone who made the rules work for them and who had a chance to get properly organized before the competition began. But was it a fair way to play the game?

3. Explain that this is like the situation in many poorer countries. Richer countries and companies are able to organize their trade (buying and selling) on a large scale so that they produce things quite cheaply; whereas local farmers often work on their own, which makes things more expensive. But aid organizations are working with local people to make things fairer. Give this example.

In the Caribbean country of Haiti, a project called Let Agogo, which means 'flowing milk', has helped farmers to organize themselves to raise money for the building of a local dairy which they can all use and in which they all share. This means that they can be much better organized and together compete on an equal basis with foreign companies.

The aid workers and local people have produced a radio advert to tell people about the milk. They encourage Haitians to 'buy local' and 'eat local'. As a result, the Let Agogo dairy products are proving a huge hit. One local farmer says: 'It seems that there is a craze for our Haitian cows' milk. Now there isn't enough milk being produced across the country to satisfy demand!'

4. Point out that aid like this is not about giving the local people milk or food. It is about working with them and ensuring that they have the resources (what they need) to work together so that they can trade and compete on a fair and equal basis.

Time for reflection

Ask the children to think about a time when someone did something that they thought was unfair. How did they feel?
Everybody wants life to be fair; we want to see justice.
What can we do today to make life more fair for other people?

Prayer

Dear God,
Thank you that you made us to work together,
to share our skills and talents for the good of everyone.
Thank you for projects like Let Agogo, which has let milk
   flow in Haiti for the benefit of the local people.
Amen.

 Class activities

1 Fair rules

Establish that trade needs fair rules – the same rules for
everyone! If this is the first time that you have talked about
trade rules with your class, do some work on why rules need
to be fair and what happens if they are not.

Talk with the children about rules in school; make a list
of these on the board. Discuss why the rules are there. What
do they think of them? What would school life be like
without them? Do they think there should be any other
rules?

Then ask each child to think up a new rule, or change one
of the existing ones so that it benefits only them. For
example, one child may change a rule about uniform:
Everyone must wear full school uniform except Rose who
can wear trainers to school. Then ask for a couple of
volunteers to come up at the front. The first child can read
out their own special rule. Ask the second child how they
would feel if that rule really existed; you could expand the
discussion to include the whole class. Then the second child
can read out their special rule; ask the first child how they
would feel if this rule was in place. This should underline the
importance of rules being fair to everyone.

Explain that there are rules covering most areas of life.
Talk about trade rules and why these need to be fair, and
need to help poor countries rather than harm them.

PSHE, Citizenship, English

2 My rule

Ask children to write a story about a day when they were allowed to introduce their own special rule to the school. Encourage them to show the consequences of that rule and how other people might respond to it.

PSHE, Citizenship, English

3 Milk

Talk about milk: where it comes from, the different types, how it is transported across the country. Set children the task of researching all the different uses of milk – which everyday foods use milk in their production and how many recipes can the children find that use milk? Do they have a favourite? Could the class cook a milk-based recipe such as microwave porridge or custard? Could they create their own milk-shakes?

Cookery, Research

4 Jigsaws

Ask the children to create images based on the assembly, perhaps focusing on Haiti, or on milk production or milk products. Use card so that the images can then be cut into pieces to make jigsaw puzzles. The children can then complete one another's puzzles.

Art and design

DISASTER!

Suitable for Whole School

 Aims

To help children understand that people in poor communities suffer disproportionately through natural disasters and to consider what can be done about this.

 Preparation and materials

- You will need an OHP, whiteboard or banner showing the words 'What a disaster!'
- Rehearse six children to take part in the sketch: four members of the Smith family, plus Sonia and the news reporter. The family should sit round a table facing a 'television screen' (a cardboard box placed at an angle so that the front is concealed from the audience). The narrator stands to one side. Sonia and the news reporter should stand on the opposite side of the space from the Smith family.
- A Bible, if you are using the story of the Good Samaritan (Luke 10.30–37).

 Assembly

1. Display the words 'What a disaster!' and ask the children, what is a disaster? Value all ideas – you could write some on the whiteboard or a flipchart.
2. Introduce the Smith family drama, saying that maybe they can help us understand a bit more about this word.

   Narrator: It is Tuesday evening and the Smith family are eating their tea.

   Sam: Something really disastrous happened today. Mrs Jones moved Laura off my table because she said

49

we were talking too much. What a disaster, I can't tell you …

Julie: (*interrupting*) That's not disastrous. Something much worse happened at football. I scored an own goal! The shame! And you should have heard Jason …

Narrator: Just then a newsflash interrupts the programme they're watching on television.

The family freezes as the reporter speaks.

Reporter: We have just received reports of a terrible earthquake in El Salvador. This is the second earthquake there in a month. It is estimated that more than 1,000 people have died and more than a million families are now homeless.

Reporter freezes.

Sam: I know all about earthquakes. You see, what happens is that rocks deep below the ground move about. It makes the ground under your feet shake so much you can't walk. (*He stands up and jiggles about.*)

Julie: It's not funny, Sam. If it's a really bad earthquake it can make whole houses fall down and kill people.

Mum: That's right, Julie. This must have been a really bad one. Can you imagine what would happen if we had an earthquake here?

Dad: No, it doesn't bear thinking about. If we had an earthquake, just think what would get damaged in this house.

Sam: Yeah. Your precious garden for a start.

Mum: Sam!

Sam: Yeah, but think about it. In this country it wouldn't be *such* a disaster. There would be plenty of people around to help us. We'd have ambulances in minutes.

Dad: And our insurance would pay for anything that was damaged.

Sam: Even your precious garden!

Julie: Hang on, there's more. Listen, they're interview-
          ing a child ...

Family freezes again.

Reporter: I have here with me Sonia Platero. Sonia, tell us
          what happened to you and your family.

Sonia: Hi, my name is Sonia Platero. I am 12 years old
          and I live in El Salvador in Central America. I have
          four sisters and one brother and live with my
          grandparents. Our house was destroyed by earth-
          quakes and we had to live in a temporary shelter
          while we tried to rebuild our home. I was inside
          the house when the second earthquake started, so I
          ran outside as quickly as I could.
             The walls were moving from side to side and it
          was very frightening. I fell over because the earth
          was moving so much – I just couldn't keep steady.
          I hurt my arm when I fell into a barbed-wire fence
          and my legs are covered in cuts and grazes.
             Our house collapsed completely and everything
          was destroyed. We managed to pull out our
          mattresses so at least we have something to sleep
          on, but everything else was broken. We are very
          poor so we can't just go and buy new things. We
          even have trouble getting water. The earthquake
          has destroyed the water system, so we have to get
          water from the river. But all our jugs are broken,
          so it is very difficult!

Sam: Makes you think, doesn't it? If we had an
          earthquake here, everyone would rush to help us
          – but they don't seem to have much help at all.

3. Explain that every year there are some small earthquakes here
   in the UK. Does anyone remember hearing about them? They
   can be a bit scary, but they don't cause much damage and
   people don't usually get hurt. In other parts of the world
   earthquakes can be much larger. Can you imagine what it
   might be like to be in an earthquake? How do you think it

would feel if all your things were broken? Disasters like that happen in different parts of the world all the time, and it is always the poorest people who are affected most. Why do you think that is?

Discuss this point, drawing out the fact that they don't have insurance, they often live in remote areas without emergency services, buildings are often not strong or are badly designed.

4. Explain that although these are serious problems they can be overcome. Let's go forward a few months and hear from Sonia again:

Sonia: My school was also destroyed and I missed going there. But a local organization has helped us rebuild our communities. It gave us advice and encouraged people to get into groups to help each other rebuild their homes. Things would have been even more difficult without its help, but now we can start again and rebuild for the future.

5. You could read or tell the Bible story of the Good Samaritan from Luke (10.30–37). Christians and many other people believe that we should do what we can to help our fellow human beings, even if they are not from our own community and even if they live a long way away. By supporting charities we can help people who suffer from disasters.

 Time for reflection

What is a disaster?

Do we sometimes use the word without thinking?

People do face real disasters in their lives – serious illness and death can happen and cause great suffering.

In this country there are natural disasters like flooding or hurricanes from time to time.

In other parts of the world there are worse natural disasters and they happen more often.

What should our response to disaster be?

Are there ways that we can help and show that we care?

Prayer

Dear God
When the earthquake has come and gone,
help me to see that it leaves behind not ruined buildings but
   ruined lives,
not ruined schools but ruined education,
not ruined water supplies but ruined health.

When the earthquake has come and gone, O God,
show me also that by working together and caring for our
   fellow human beings,
there is hope even in the darkest times.
Amen.

 Class activities

1 Mind maps

Discuss with the class what they understand about disasters.
Write the word 'Disaster' in the middle of one half of the
board. Create a mind map around the word, writing down
all the things that children associate with disaster, including
their feelings about it. Make connections between the words,
perhaps linking events to feeling words or grouping together
natural disasters or personal disasters.

   Do the same on the other half of the board with the word
'Hope', writing down the thoughts and feelings that children
associate with the word. Compare your two mind maps.

   Read Sonia's story to the class. How has the disaster
affected her life? Having listened to the story, add more
words to your disaster mind map. What gives Sonia hope
that things will change for the better? How are charities
helping? Add the words from your discussion to the hope
mind map.

English, PSHE

2 Poetry

Ask the children to write a poem on the theme of disaster
and how Sonia might have felt. They could write an acrostic

poem, using the initial letters of the word 'disaster'. Or they could write a cinquaine – a five-line poem where the first line has one word, the second line has two words, the third has three, the fourth has two and the final line has one, as in the following example:

disaster,
brings despair,
makes lives desperate,
until someone
helps

English

3 Collage

Create a collage continuum to represent hope. Two groups work together on a large piece of paper. One group starts in a corner representing 'disaster'. The other group starts in the opposite corner representing 'hope'. They then create a collage of pictures, colours, words and symbols, cut out or torn from magazines, depicting a continuum or journey from disaster to hope.

Before starting work, talk together about what the appropriate images and words might be; also think about the colours used at each end and where and how disaster and hope will meet in the middle.

Art and design

4 Display and assembly

Display the mind maps, poems and collages you have created, either in the classroom or in a school corridor, to inform others about what you have learnt. You could base an assembly on this work.

Presentation skills

SMALL STEPS AND GIANT LEAPS

Suitable for Whole School

 Aims

To suggest that human beings, working together, can overcome any problem, including the challenges of global poverty and climate change.

 Preparation and materials

- None required.

 Assembly

1. Begin by reading the words below, adapted from a speech President Kennedy made in 1961.

   > I believe that this nation should commit itself to achieving the goal, before this decade is out, of eating a piece of pie. No single project in this period will be more impressive to mankind, or more important; and none will be so difficult or expensive to accomplish.

   Ask the children what is wrong with what you've just read and if any of them know what should be in the place of 'eating a piece of pie'. Explain that the speech was given by US President John F. Kennedy in 1961 and was about landing a man on the moon. This is what he really said:

   > I believe that this nation should commit itself to achieving the goal, before this decade is out, of landing a man on the

Moon and returning him safely to the Earth. No single space project in this period will be more impressive to mankind or more important for the long-range exploration of space; and none will be so difficult or expensive to accomplish.

2. Explain that within nine years, in July 1969, two Americans did land on the moon. Ask if anyone knows their names (Neil Armstrong and Buzz Aldrin). What about the name of the vital third crew member who stayed in lunar orbit (circling the moon)? He was Michael Collins.

    They had done it! It took an amazing effort, billions of dollars, and even cost the lives of a number of astronauts who died in training. Scientists and engineers developed new metal alloys, new fuels, and amazing new technology to do things that no one had ever done before; no one knew if it was even possible to fly to the moon, land there and come home safely!

3. President Kennedy's words became famous; but even more famous were the words of Neil Armstrong when he stepped on to the moon: 'That's one small step for (a) man; one giant leap for mankind.' (For accuracy you might want to mention that Armstrong thinks he said 'a' but that it is lost in the static – but this point is not relevant to the assembly.)

4. The day before the successful Apollo 11 mission was launched, there was a protest at the launch site led by the Reverend Ralph Abernathy. Several hundred members of the Poor People's Campaign were upset that so many billions were being spent on space exploration while they and millions of others lived in poverty. They wanted the money spent on the basics of life: food for the hungry, clothing, housing and medical care.

    The boss of NASA (the American Space Agency), Thomas Paine, met Ralph Abernathy and said to him: 'If we could solve the problems of poverty by not pushing the button to launch men to the moon tomorrow, then we would not push that button.'

5. People can argue about whether or not it was right to go to the moon, but it did show one thing: people can achieve what seems impossible but they need four things:

- The will – determination to solve the problems and not give up.
- Team work – thousands of people worked on the moon landings and every one of them was vital.
- Ingenuity – the amazing creative abilities of human beings.
- Resources – basically the money needed to get the job done.

6. If you were writing a speech today like President Kennedy's what would you believe the nation, the European Union or the world should commit to, within ten years: cheap sustainable energy for the world, an end to hunger around the world, basic medical care for everyone, education for all children, an end to child labour … ?

   These may seem huge tasks but if human beings went to the moon, can't we tackle these big problems back on earth?

 ## Time for reflection

I believe that this nation/this Union/this world should commit itself to achieving the goal before this decade is out of … what? What would you like to see a big commitment to?

 ## Prayer

Dear God,
We thank you for the inspiration of people who achieve great things.
Help us to think big about what we can achieve if we really want to.
Amen.

 ## Class activities

1 Debate
Was it right to spend so much money going to the moon when many Americans were – and still are – so poor? Discuss this, perhaps even holding a formal debate. The following is some background information.

- Many Americans lived in great poverty at the time.
- Most poor people had very limited healthcare and children often died because of the inadequate medical system.
- The problems of poverty hit the black population to a greater extent than they did the white.
- Very few black people were employed in the space programme.
- The money for the space programme came from different budgets and it would have been hard to move it to poverty programmes.
- Landing on the moon was inspirational for the whole world.
- The space programme created thousands of jobs.
- Pictures of the earth from space have played an important part in the worldwide ecology movement.
- Advances in science made for the moon landing have helped improve other aspects of our lives.

Children can research further background information to support their arguments.

English, Research, History

2 'I believe ... ' statements

Ask children to create their own statements based on Kennedy's speech. What would they like to see a big commitment to? You could discuss why some projects seem to attract more interest than others. Would it be best to go for a technology project such as developing sources of sustainable energy?

English

3 Campaign

Talk about any campaigns that the children have heard of, such as Make Poverty History or Comic Relief. How do campaigns happen? What are the elements of a good campaign? Talk about publicity, letter-writing, meetings, etc.

Would the class, and perhaps the school, like to take one of the 'I believe' statements and use it to begin a campaign?

Perhaps they could write to their MEP using a letter like this:

> We believe that the nations of this Union should commit themselves to achieving the goal, within ten years, of developing cheap, safe, non-polluting energy for the world. No single project in this period will be more impressive or more important for the long-term development of humankind and peace among nations; and none will be so difficult or expensive to accomplish, requiring us to work together for the good of all.

English

4 Earth images

Create an image of the earth as if you are looking from the moon, with the title 'Look after this planet'. You could use chalk on black paper or a collage approach to get the high contrast between the bright surface of the moon, the darkness of the sky and the rich blues and whites of the earth.

Art

Section 2
Food, water and shelter for all

WIGGLY WORMS AND FERTILIZED FOOD

Suitable for Whole School

Aims

To understand how a small change can make a big difference, applying this to development issues and children's own experience.

Preparation and materials

- The assembly begins with some worms! You could dig up some worms and bring them in a container, or get a wormery which could then stay in school as a reminder of the assembly. Or you could use artificial worms, either from a toy shop or from a fishing fan (they make their own using moulds – make sure you get some without hooks!). Alternatively use worm-shaped sweets.
- Use rubber gloves, even if the worms aren't real, just to make the health and safety point. Lightweight gloves (such as latex) provide protection and give a more sensitive touch for picking up wriggly things!
- You will also need a bag of garden waste and/or fruit and veg left-overs. Make sure it's not too ripe and you'll need the gloves again here.
- If you include a song in your assembly, two that mention worms are 'If I were a butterfly' (*Come and Praise*, BBC), and 'Wiggly Waggly Song' (*Come and Praise Beginning*, BBC).

Assembly

1. Show your worms and invite the children, one at a time, to come and pick one up using a glove. (Judge your audience, as

this can be a very excitable beginning to the assembly! You may prefer to do the picking up yourself, which will probably produce plenty of excitement anyway.) If you are using toy worms you could take a handful out of your pocket in a very casual manner, giving them a shake to make them wriggle.

2. Ask the children what they think worms are good for. Elicit responses that include the following or make these points yourself:

   - They're good just for being themselves! They don't need to have a purpose that suits us!
   - They help to break up the soil, making it easier for plants to grow.
   - They provide food for birds (although the worms themselves might not think this is 'good'!).

3. Explain that there is something else that worms do that makes a big difference to the lives of many people around the world. Today we are going to focus on a part of the world called the Philippines. Ask if anyone has heard of the Philippines, and value any information given.

   Present the following facts. You could prime children to present these facts, perhaps with large cards or using a PowerPoint or other presentation. It is important to keep it fast-moving at this point as facts about the Philippines are not the main focus of the assembly.

   - Show the location of the Philippines on a map (Western Pacific).
   - The country is made up of more than 7,000 small islands.
   - Fifty-five per cent of people speak Filipino and there are other local languages; 45 per cent can speak English.
   - Nearly half the people in the Philippines live on about £1 a day – so there is a lot of poverty and people struggle to live.

   If you have time you could run a quick quiz on these facts.

4. Now back to the worms – what on earth could worms have to do with the Philippines? Explain that the answer is in your bag. Show the bag, asking if anyone is brave enough to put their hand in here and pull out what's in it – especially after

the worms at the start of the assembly! Add to the tension by saying that they will need to wear a rubber glove for this too. (As with the advice above about excitement, you may judge it best to do this yourself.)

5. Show the vegetation in the bag and ask the children what will happen to it if it is left lying around? It will rot and go bad. This was what was happening to rubbish in the Philippines until a local organization got the bright idea of giving the farmers there ... can you guess? A kilo, a whole kilo of wriggling, squiggling worms!

Explain that the worms eat the rotting vegetation and left-overs, so that's one job done. But at the same time they produce natural compost (from worm casts – you've probably seen them on the ground, little brown squiggly cones), which make excellent fertilizer (plant food). The fertilizer helps crops to grow better: bigger and stronger. And the great thing is, once a farmer has his or her worms, worms make more worms to make more worm casts to go on making better crops. So the farmers don't need to borrow money to buy expensive fertilizer, and their crops are better, so they make more money for themselves – all with the help of a few, happy, well-fed worms that clear up the rubbish! Plus the crops are healthier to eat, making the whole family healthier too. Not bad.

6. End by pointing out that sometimes a little, simple idea can have a big impact.

 Time for reflection

Think about those worms in the Philippines.
Who would have thought that such a tiny thing as a worm could do such a big job!
Are there small changes that you could make in your life?
Perhaps you could say a kind word to someone, or set aside just a few minutes for some extra school work or to help at home, or use the internet to find out more about how small ideas can help farmers in countries all over the world.

Prayer

Dear God,
Thank you for worms and the difference they are making to
lives in the Philippines.
Thank you for the wonders of the natural world
and the way that things work together for good – especially
worms!
Amen.

 Class activities

1 A worm card

Make a 'worm card' – a fold-over card (like a birthday card)
with an illustration of wiggly worms on the front. Inside the
card, each child writes down one small way in which they
can make a difference: do better at school, be more helpful
and friendly. What small thing will you do today?

PSHE, Citizenship

2 Make it clear

Photocopy the 'Make it clear' worksheet (page 66) for use
with older children, to help them make sense of the
difficulties faced by farmers in the Philippines and elsewhere.
Cut up the squares, and the task is to arrange them in the
right order.
(Answers: 1F; 2C; 3B; 4G; 5H; 6A; 7D; 8E)

PSHE, Citizenship, Logical thinking skills – sequencing

3 Calculation activities

Calculate these problems based around the situation.

Pamfilo is a farmer in the Philippines. His field needs 250 kg
of compost (made by worms) to help the plants grow well.
Compost is packed in 50 kg bags. How many bags of
compost does he need to cover his field?
(Answer: 5 bags)

Make it clear

A Now the farmers use worms to make excellent natural fertilizer (which is much cheaper).

B The Filipino government lends farmers money to buy fertilizers and rice seeds from abroad.

C This is because their crops don't always grow well and they don't get paid much for them.

D The crops give the farmers much better harvests.

E The farmers have more crops to sell so they can make more money, which can be used to send their children to school.

F It can be hard for farmers to make a living in the Philippines.

G The farmers have to pay the government back though, so they don't make much money.

H The farmers sometimes need a helping hand. A local organization, RDI Leyte, can help with:
- worms
- local knowledge
- training.

Views from different faiths on economic and social justice

'Happy are those who risk
danger to do what is right;
they know what it is to live
in God's kingdom.'

Matthew 5.10 (Christianity)

'God requires justice and
kindness and giving...'

The Qur'an 16.90 (Islam)

'My religion is simple. My religion is
kindness. If you can help others, it is
very good. Yet if you cannot do this,
at least do not harm them.'

H H the Dalai Lama (Buddhism)

'If everybody took enough for their
own needs and nothing more, there
would be no poverty in this world.'

Mahatma Gandhi (Hinduism)

'Woe to him who builds his house by
unrighteousness, and his upper rooms
by injustice; who makes his neighbours
work for nothing, and does not give
them their wages.'

Jeremiah 22.13 (Judaism)

'Production and trade in
business are all done as part
of an honest religious life.'

Dharam di Kirt (Sikhism)

It takes Pamfilo's family one and a half days to make 4 bags of compost. How many bags can they make in:

(a) One week?
(b) Two weeks?
(c) Ten weeks?

Note that Pamfilo and his family do not work on Sundays as they go to church.
(Answers: (a) 16 bags; (b) 32 bags; (c) 160 bags)

And how many kg does that make?
(Answers: (a) 800 kg; (b) 1,600 kg; (c) 8,000 kg)

Maths

4 Views from different faiths
Copy the faith quotes on economic and social justice from the worksheet (see page 67). Ask children to reflect on different faiths' understanding of justice. Which is their favourite quote and why?

PSHE, Citizenship, RE

BIG FAT JUICY SNAILS – YUM!

Suitable for Whole School

 Aims

To increase children's understanding of people's need for fair access to food.

 Preparation and materials

- You will need a tin of snails (available from delicatessens).
- Optional: An opaque bag containing sweets – important that their size and shape seen through the bag could suggest chunks of giant snail meat, for example, pineapple chunk sweets or something similar.

 Assembly

1. Introduce the theme of food. Ask the children to guess what foods you are describing:

   - Cold, creamy, sweet, great in summer, sometimes comes in a cone (ice cream).
   - Dark or light brown, sometimes white, comes in bars, most people love it (chocolate).
   - Good meat and tastes sweet …

   Those children who eat meat will probably have suggestions. Accept them all, but then explain that this is a direct quote from a 14-year-old boy in the African country of Ghana. Ask the children to guess the animal he's talking about from the following clues:

   - It has no legs.
   - Lives on the land.
   - It has a hard protective shell.

- Its name rhymes with a type of bird beginning with Q ... quail ... snail!

Allow for the expected expressions of revulsion.

Optional: Then say that you have some snail meat here, would anyone like to try it? Produce the bag of sweets from your pocket and offer them round, enjoying the joke if someone is brave enough to put their hand in the bag and pull one out.

2. Show the tinned snails and explain that many people consider snails a great delicacy, particularly in France and in the most expensive restaurants in this country. Use this as an opportunity to explore the idea that not everyone likes the same things to eat and that we often find other people's tastes strange just because it is not what we're used to. You could mention any particular food dislikes of your own and ask children to share theirs.

   (It is important here to avoid any feeling that snails are 'OK for poor people in poor countries' who can't get 'proper' food. Explain that there is no such thing as 'proper' food and that 'one man's meat is another man's poison' or, in a more modern version, 'one person's delicious steak is a vegetarian's murdered animal'!)

3. Tell the story of how Gideon and Timothy in Ghana came to be eating snail meat.

Gideon is 11 and his best friend is Timothy, who is 14. They live in a village in Ghana, which is a country in Africa. The boys' families are farmers. They used to grow cassava and maize, but a few years ago, their landlord said everyone would have to pay more for the land. Gideon's dad, Moses, and Timothy's dad, Mathias, couldn't afford to pay. So the landlord took their land, and sold some of it to a big company that grew pineapples. The families could no longer grow food for themselves. They didn't have enough money to buy food. Gideon and Timothy had to stop going to school because they couldn't pay the fees. They were very unhappy.

Then they heard about the Development Action Association (DAA), which had an unusual idea to help people get the food they needed. The DAA showed people how to breed giant African land snails. It has a 'snail bank', and Moses was given 168 snails. These snails can grow to be as long as 20cm! Once his snails had produced lots of baby snails, Moses gave some back to the snail bank so someone else could start snail farming.

Timothy's dad Mathias also keeps snails now. Timothy says, 'Before, we could not always get food. Now we can eat snails every day. It is good meat and tastes sweet.'

Gideon and Timothy help to look after the snails. Gideon says, 'I feed the snails, water them, sweep the room and wash their feeding trays. They help our family get money and they taste nice.' Sometimes the boys help to collect the snails ready to sell at market.

Gideon and Timothy are looking forward to the future. Timothy wants to be a taxi driver when he grows up, but Gideon can't decide. Perhaps he will be a snail farmer, or drive a lorry, or, best of all, be a footballer!

4. Timothy and Gideon would never have dreamed of eating snails if the Development Action Association hadn't come along with a new and clever idea. All over the world people are finding new ways to live. We're having to find some ourselves too, because of climate change. When the boys' families lost their land they needed to find a new idea, but was it fair that the land was taken from them in the first place?

 Time for reflection

Think about those snails.
Does it seem strange to you to eat snail meat?
Can you see that some of the things that you eat will seem strange to people in other countries?
Many British people eat sausages, which people in some other countries think are awful.
Many people around the world eat meat, while vegetarians and vegans find it hard to even think of eating dead animals!
Is it important to you that everyone in the world has enough to eat and is treated fairly?

If appropriate, include these short readings:

> The kind of fasting I want is this: remove the chains of oppression and the yoke of injustice, and let the oppressed go free. Share your food with the hungry and open your homes to the homeless poor. Give clothes to those who have nothing to wear, and do not refuse to help your own relatives. (Bible, Isaiah 58.6–7, GNB)

> If you see an evil action, change it with your hand, if you are not able to do this, then with your tongue, if you are not able to do it, then with your heart. (Muslim Hadith)

> This world is the home of God. He dwells in all things. One should only take what one needs and leave the rest for others, because it really all belongs to God. (Hindu Isa Upanishad)

 ## Prayer

I think of all the food that I can enjoy.
I think of people who don't have enough food.
Dear God, help us all to make your world a fairer place.
Amen.

 ## Song

This is best if practised with a group of children beforehand, but could probably be done from scratch. Sing to the tune of 'The Farmer's in his Den', and add in appropriate actions.

1 The farmer's in his field
The farmer's in his field
E – I – E – I
The farmer's in his field.

2 The farmers grow their crops ...

3 They have to leave the land ...

4 It's hard to find food ...

5 They start to farm some snails ...

6 There's now more food to eat ...

7 God help us all to care
God help us all to share
E – I – E – I
God help us to be fair.

Class activities

1 What do you know?

Give groups copies of the story of Gideon and Timothy to read. Ask the children to devise questions for further research. For example, what they would like to ask the two friends, the landowner and the workers at DAA, and what they would like to ask about Ghana. Groups report back to the rest of the class. Focus on the reasons for the problem: why the landlord set such high rates and why the DAA is trying to find people employment in their own community.

Share the resulting questions, and let groups interview one another to see what answers they can come up with.

Geography, English, PSHE, Citizenship

2 Our favourite foods survey

Conduct a class survey to find out what the children's favourite foods are. This information could be presented in a variety of charts. You could also make the survey wider, perhaps by asking other classes or teachers for their opinions.

Science, Maths

3 Snail prayers

Ask the class to write prayers in a swirling snail shell shape, starting in the middle of a page and twirling round and round. They could be prayers of thanksgiving for the food we enjoy, prayers for Timothy and Gideon, prayers for those in the world who don't have enough to eat. If this activity takes place in advance of the assembly, some prayers could be read out or on display as children leave the assembly space.

RE

4 Snail and bugs café

Research edible bugs – things that we would not normally eat but which are perfectly nutritious foods, perhaps even tasty! Write the menu for a café that serves snails and bugs in appetizing dishes. You could also decorate your menu in an attractive style.

English, Art and design, Cookery

WATER

Suitable for Whole School

 ### Aims

To help children understand the importance of water and how having access to clean water improves people's lives dramatically.

 ### Preparation and materials

- Only undertake this assembly if you are game for getting wet!
- You will need some sort of water squirter (not of the super-soaker type!); perhaps just a squeezy bottle, to avoid the connotation of weapons.
- Waterproof clothing for yourself – including goggles and a hat if you choose!
- You may need to stand on something waterproof such as a plastic mat, and have a mop handy for after the assembly. In summer you could do the whole thing outside.
- You will need the following items, covered with a cloth at the start of the assembly: dry crackers; a jug of water; tumblers to drink from; an umbrella.
- Ask a child to read Saida's story.
- Optional: A map showing Peru (atlas or whiteboard).

 ### Assembly

1. Explain that under the cloth you have the most precious, important and valuable thing in the world. Ask for suggestions as to what it might be, then remove the cloth and explain that the assembly is all about this important substance: water.

   Ask them if they expected it to be water. Why or why not? Do they think water is valuable? Why or why not?

2. Produce your water squirter and explain that you wanted to make sure that they remember how important water is, so you've come up with this idea.

   Every time you say the word 'water' – and only that word – you want someone to spray you with the water squirter. Choose your volunteer carefully (perhaps picking them in advance); you want someone who will follow the rules. You could ask another member of staff to do the water squirting.

   Put on your protective clothing to heighten the drama. As you do so, be crystal clear about the rules: the volunteer can only spray when you say the particular word you mentioned before, and they can only spray in the agreed direction at the agreed target (you).

3. Begin by asking the children for suggestions of what we need **water** for. Ask a child to eat three crackers without **water** – is it easy? Give the volunteer a drink of **water** when they have finished.

   Show the umbrella, saying that we live in a country where it rains a lot. That's why lots of people own one of these – to keep the rain**water** off us. You might attempt to deflect the spray with a quick flourish of the umbrella at this point.

   And it's easy for us to drink lots of **water** and fill up lots of glasses like this from the tap.

   Say that you've had enough spraying for now, and the game is definitely over! Ask your volunteer to sit down but to remain nearby (they can give one last squirt at the end of the assembly).

4. Explain that people living in other countries often have to travel a long way to get enough water for themselves, and for their animals and plants. They may walk for miles to get to it, and then once they've collected it they have to carry it all the way back home. It is very hard work – the water is heavy and sometimes the people get tired and spill some.

   This is what life used to be like for a girl called Saida and her family, who live in Peru – you could show this on an atlas or whiteboard map. Ask your reader to tell Saida's story.

Do you ever help to water your garden? I do! My name is Saida and I am eight years old. I live in a small village in the mountains in a country called Peru. I live with my mum, dad, my brother and my two sisters.

I like helping my dad in our garden. We grow all sorts of vegetables. We didn't have a garden before. But now we've got cabbages, garlic, onions, lettuces, parsley and oregano. All sorts! It is really easy to water the garden now because we've got a tap in our house. You see, until a couple of years ago, my mum had to go and collect water from a pond whenever we needed it. It was very tiring for her as the buckets of water were heavy. Also, the water in the pond isn't very clean so we used to get sick from drinking it.

Then my dad and some other people in the village contacted a local organization working in the area and asked if it could help us. They help bring change to make life better for families like mine. The people from the organization came and showed my dad and others in the village how to put in water pipes and taps. They also taught us how to look after the water and keep it clean. Dad worked hard to put the pipes in and he also dug into the ground to build a new toilet. He recently put in a new sink too!

The first day we had running water at home was so exciting. My sister, friends and I had a shower under the tap. Mum was so happy. She doesn't have to walk for ages with buckets to fetch water now. It's right here! She has more time to cook dinner and it's easy to prepare the vegetables.

5. Think about how lucky we are in this country. All we have to do is turn on a tap to get water. But only about 15 per cent of people in the world have taps in their homes. Ask seven children to come to the front and stand in a row. Ask one to step forward, to illustrate this statistic. That's only about one in every seven people. That means that the majority of people in the world have to walk to fetch water and carry it back home again. Point to the other six. And most of those people live in hot, dry countries.

The good news is that it does not have to be this way, and these six can get water on tap if they get some help to build pipes and wells. Charities and local organizations work with people in these countries to try to make sure that everyone can have clean water. But the charities need some help to do this. How do you think we can help? Think about it and tell your teacher when you get back to the classroom.

Ask if the children would like you to go back to being squirted every time you say the W word?

When this is agreed, say that the next time they turn on a tap, they should remember that the most valuable thing in the world is coming out. Pause and look at the water squirter, then say: 'And that's **water.**'

Time for reflection

Ensure that there is a break in the assembly at this point. Ask your water squirter to sit down and make it clear to everyone that the water squirting is now finished and you need them to settle down before you move into the more reflective part of the assembly.

Ask the children to close their eyes for a moment and imagine this:

It's a really hot summer's day and you've been outside playing all morning.

You've been running around and you're tired. You need a drink.

You go inside, but there's nothing to drink.

You've got to walk for an hour to go and fetch some water. How do you feel?

Now imagine that it's the same day and you go inside and there's a tap!

You turn on the tap and cold, fresh water comes out.

You have a long drink. How do you feel now?

Prayer

Thank you, God, that we live in a place where we have clean, fresh water in our homes.

Let's not take this for granted and let's remember others who don't have enough water.

Thank you for charities in this country working with people in other countries to provide clean water for everyone.

Amen.

Class activities

1 Think back

Ask the class to think back to the last time they used water. What was it for? Ask for some suggestions. Maybe it was to have a drink at breaktime, or when they washed their hands or brushed their teeth, or when they gave their dog some water before school.

Now ask them to think about all the things they could not do at home if they did not have water. Make a class list on the board; ensure that fun things such as water fights are included, as well as everyday actions like washing up, cooking, drinking, etc.

Leave the list on the board while you do the other activities below.

PSHE

2 Drawing Saida

Read Saida's story to the class and ask what things Saida can do now she has a tap in her home that she couldn't do before.

Ask the children to draw an outline of a person to represent Saida. Write words outside her outline that describe what her life was like and how she might have felt before she had water in her home. Then write inside the outline words that describe what life is like for Saida now and how the children think she might feel now her family has a tap.

You can do this as a whole class activity, using a large sheet and drawing round someone to create the outline. Children can write their words on pieces of paper and stick them on the outline.

PSHE, English, Art and design

3 Proande

Tell the class that the organization that helped Saida's family get their tap was called Proande. The people who live in Saida's village had been very unhappy because the government in Peru would not pay to put in pipes and taps for them to have water, so they decided to do something about it themselves. They went and asked Proande to show them how to install a water system and taps. Proande agreed, and so the villagers and Proande worked together to get the job done. Proande was able to buy many of the materials they needed because a charity in the UK gave some money to help.

Ask the children if they think that's a good way of working. Why or why not? How would they do things differently?

4 Workshops

Tell the class that at her school Saida has lessons about hygiene and how to keep the water in her village clean. These lessons are called workshops and use lots of pictures and different visual ways of teaching the children about when they should wash their hands and where they should get their water from.

Split the class into small groups and ask each one to come up with a subject linked to water that they will run a short workshop about (no more than ten minutes). They might choose how to use water wisely in school; the importance of washing your hands; showing new pupils where they can get a drink and find the toilet; or something they learnt about in the previous activity. The children should spend some time planning their workshop, perhaps using the following questions as guidelines.

- What is your workshop going to be about?
- What information do you want people to know at the end of it?
- How will you tell your audience this information? (Explain it to them; show them by acting it out; give them something to take away to remind them about what they have learnt.)
- How will you check that they have understood what you have told them? (Perhaps hold a quiz or ask someone to show you what you've been explaining.)

Allow the groups to practise their workshops before showing them to the rest of the class. The workshops could be presented to other classes; or hold an assembly to tell the rest of the school all that you have learnt.

English, Study skills

5 Posters

Make posters about using water wisely and why water is so valuable. If possible, laminate the best ones and display them around school, near taps and other places where water is used.

PSHE, Citizenship, Art and design

TOMATO

Suitable for Whole School

 ### Aims

To show that helping people in a small way can have a big impact and that everyone can make a difference.

 ### Preparation and materials

- Think of some suitable subjects for the Tomato Game.
- Prepare one or more readers for Rosa's story or be ready to read or paraphrase it yourself.

 ### Assembly

1. Introduce your Tomato Game and explain the rules. You are going to think of something and begin to describe it but instead of using the proper word you'll say 'Tomato'. So if you were thinking of a prince, you might say, 'Have you read Harry Potter and the Half-Blood TOMATO?'

   Every few sentences you will pause and ask the children to put their hands up (but not to shout out) if they think they know what you are thinking of.

2. Play the game. For example:

   I bought a new TOMATO the other day. It's bright red. I looked at a blue one but decided I liked the red one better.

   Pause; some hands might go up.

   The lady who sold it to me said that she had a TOMATO just like it and her children think it is great. They particularly like the built-in MP3 player.

   Pause

I decided to go for the option of a metallic colour and having some stripes down the side of my TOMATO.

Pause

I went for the fuel-efficient, energy-saving TOMATO, to help the environment and save me money, because I pay a lower TOMATO tax every year.

Pause

I like my new TOMATO. It has four doors and a hatchback, and horn that goes PIP PIP.

Everyone's hands should be up!

Play the game a few times with your own subjects, with your clues starting difficult and getting easier.

3. End with a one-sentence version of the game: The thing that changed my life completely was a TOMATO! Go on to explain that in this case it really was tomatoes that made a big difference. Introduce Rosa's story and ask your reader to begin.

My name is Rosa Estepan. I live in a place called Ojer Kaibal, which is a small village in Guatemala, which is a country in Central America close to Mexico.

I am 33 years old and have five children. My youngest child is 3 and the oldest is 13. Perhaps some of you come from a similar-sized family, but probably only a few of you!

It is hot and dry where we live and many people are very poor. A few years ago my husband and I were struggling to make enough money to send our children to school and buy medicines if they were ill. But today, thanks to the help of a local organization, all that has changed.

About four years ago, a local organization lent me some money to buy tomato seeds so that I could grow the tomato plants and sell the fruit. I made a little more money than the amount of the loan, so at the end of the year I was able to pay the organization what I owed them. The next year they lent me a bit more money, so I was able to buy more seeds and some fertilizer. Now I grow beans and maize too.

We eat some of our crops and sell the rest. This means that we now have enough money to buy other food, and clothes for the children. As well as the loan, they have taught me how to grow crops well and how to look after animals.

4. Things have changed so much for Rosa. It's just like the tomato seeds: from one seed a whole bush grows – and from the small loan her whole life has grown better. Stress that the help that Rosa received was what's called 'seed funding'. It's not an endless payment, just a small loan to get her started, which she paid back. It is all about helping people who do most of the work themselves. Rosa's tomatoes show us that giving just a little money in this country can make a big difference in someone's life. We can all help to make a difference. Who'd have thought that tomatoes could change a family's life!

 ## Time for reflection

Do you like tomatoes?
Do you like them on pizza, or as a pasta sauce, or as ketchup on your chips?
Perhaps you don't like to eat tomatoes.
That's not important, but think about a tomato:
It's a fruit, though we eat it like a vegetable.
It's a beautiful, bright red colour.
It's full of seeds, so one makes many more.
It can make a big, big difference to people's lives, as we've heard.
Not bad for one little fruit?

 ## Prayer

Dear God,
Thank you for the wonderful variety of growing things that the world provides.
And thank you for the inspiring story of Rosa,
and everyone who grows hope out of the smallest thing.
Amen.

End the assembly by saying: 'Now it's time to go back to your TOMATO rooms and get on with the rest of your day. So leading out, we'll have this TOMATO leaving first ... '

 ## Class activities

1 Tomato Game

Play the Tomato Game in class, first altogether and then in pairs. This requires children to think about the language they are using. It is a great mind-gym type exercise requiring quick thinking and a fun competitive element.

English, Creative thinking

2 Where in the world?

Ask children what they know about Central America and in particular the country of Guatemala. Split the class into small groups and give each one different resources. Ask them to come up with a list of ten facts about Guatemala. The resources could be books containing appropriate information, access to or copies of web material, etc. Join the groups together and share facts in order to come up with a class list of information about Guatemala. Display your list in the classroom.

You could hold a Guatemala quiz using the information collected, with children working in pub-quiz-type teams.

Geography, Research skills

3 Just tomatoes?

As a class, read Rosa's story. Rosa grew tomatoes in order to make some money for food and clothes for her family. Based on what the children have found out about Guatemala, discuss what other things Rosa or someone from her village could use a loan for. The class could split into small groups, each coming up with a suggestion about how one of the villagers could use a loan to make their life better. Group suggestions could then be reported back to the class or written up as a project.

English, Geography

4 How can we help?

The concept behind the scheme in Rosa's village is very simple – by helping someone in even a small way, they may be able to change their whole life. Ask the class for ideas of things that they could do to help other people in:

- their school
- their town
- the world.

Each child could then choose one idea and write up how it could help other people and the effect it might have. They could illustrate the process with a diagram or flow chart.

Challenge the children to turn some of the ideas into action. Help them to see that they too can play a part in making the world a better place.

PSHE, Citizenship

RED HOT CHILLIES, RED HOT EXPERTS!

Suitable for Whole School

 Aims

To understand the value of experts and local knowledge.

 Preparation and materials

- You will need four packets of crisps of different flavours; four scarves or pieces of cloth suitable for blindfolds; four chairs.
- A responsible adult helper.
- Three children to read Suriya's story: one as narrator and two to read what Johnny and Suriya say – or read this yourself.
- Before the assembly, carefully open the four packets of crisps and swap the contents so that, for example, the salt and vinegar crisps are in the cheese and onion packet.

 Assembly

1. Start by asking the children if they know what the word 'expert' means. Explain that today you need to find some expert crisp tasters. Maybe there are some here in the assembly who know a thing or two about crisps. Choose four volunteers but stress that everyone will be involved in trying to be a crisp expert – or 'crispert'!

   Sit the four volunteers on the chairs and blindfold them carefully. Produce the crisps and give one packet to each child. Ask each in turn to taste their crisps and say what flavour they are. They will, of course, give the 'wrong' answer as far as the audience is concerned, and there will probably be a good deal of laughter. Remove the blindfolds, and explain the trick you played. Ask the watching children if they believed that they knew better than the tasters. Ask them who were the real experts, the blindfolded crisp tasters, or those watching them.

2. Ask if anyone has ever eaten chilli-flavoured crisps. What are chillies? Has anyone ever eaten a raw chilli? Make the point that they are very spicy. Introduce the story by explaining that it is about someone who grows very strong, hot chillies. Her name is Suriya Begum.

Suriya Begum lives in a village in Bangladesh. Most people in Bangladesh are farmers. Many schools in the UK and Ireland have a harvest festival and decorate their halls with vegetables such as carrots, onions and marrows that have been grown for us by farmers. But Suriya harvests a different type of crop – red-hot chillies!

Chillies are great for people who like hot and spicy food. Suriya has grown chillies for many years, but it hasn't always been easy. Farmers like Suriya were told that they would grow more food if they bought expensive foreign seeds and used chemical fertilizer. But Suriya explains what happened: 'We just grew more weeds!'

Luckily, a local organization was able to help Suriya and the other farmers, teaching them how to grow plants without using chemicals. Johnny, who works for them, says: 'We compost leaves or use them as mulch to help return the goodness to the soil. We're not against modern science, but we are trying to make the most of local knowledge.'

Mulch, compost and natural fertilizers, such as animal manure, help the soil keep in moisture. Farmers have found that vegetable seeds planted without adding chemicals actually grow better, and the vegetables taste better too! What's more, using these natural products rather than chemical fertilizer is much better for the environment. The chemical fertilizer killed off some types of wild plants, and fish died in the rivers, so it wasn't just the farmers whose lives got better as a result of using natural fertilizers.

Suriya also visited the organization's seed store and found that she had thousands of seeds to choose from. Johnny told her: 'Here, we keep 3,000 different types of seed.'

So what did Suriya pick? Chillies! Suriya says: 'I like harvesting chillies, and our crops fetch good prices. There is a lot of bending down involved, but I don't mind. I have been doing it since I was a child.'

And Suriya is proud of her organic chillies.

'I think they're so good because I do not use chemical fertilizer. My chillies are so hot that you cannot eat even one raw!'

3. Explain that many people in Bangladesh work as farmers, so the land is very important to them. They know a lot about different kinds of soil, and which types of plant grow best in different spots. They have an amazing variety of kinds of vegetables, with names you may never have heard of, such as lady's finger and jackfruit.

   For hundreds of years, seeds have been passed from person to person. But Suriya and the farmers where she lives were told to buy seeds from foreign businesses that they couldn't really afford, and sometimes the seeds didn't grow as well as the types of seeds they had been using for years.

   Ask the children who they think the experts in the story were. Why did they know best? Stress the value of local knowledge and the experience of people who have done a job for a long time.

4. You could end the assembly by allowing children to take a few crisps each as they leave, if this is appropriate to the school's nutrition policy.

   Alternatively try apple or vegetable crisps and relate this to the point about the wide variety of vegetables that Bangladeshi farmers grow.

 ## Time for reflection

Chillies are hot –
sometimes too hot to eat.
Experts are hot – hot on their subject.
But no expert is too hot to listen and to learn from others.

Prayer

Today we are going to use our hands to help us pray. Clench your fingers and turn your hands so you do a 'thumbs down'.

> Let's remember times when we have been selfish and ungrateful for our food and the good things we have.

Slowly raise your thumbs so that you are doing a 'thumbs up'.

> As we do this, let us thank God for the food that grows and for people like Suriya who grow good food for us to eat.

Move your thumbs together.

> Let's pray for our friends, our families, and those we are close to.
>
> **Amen.**

Class activities

1 What is an expert?

Discuss the notion of experts and expertise: when we need help, we have to ask people who know what to do. An expert is someone who knows how to help people. We can all be experts at something, no matter how young or old we are. Working in pairs, ask the children to tell each other what they are good at doing.

Citizenship, PSHE

2 Expert words

Ask the children who we ask to help us when:

- We need to have our eyes tested.
- We have a burst pipe that needs mending.
- We need our teeth checked.
- We need help with our maths homework.
- We have a broken leg.

You could develop this into a pub-quiz-type activity with teams of children writing their answers down. You could add some more tricky questions, such as:

- Who do we go to for help if we are going bald? (Trichologist)
- What is a bell-ringer properly called? (Campanologist)
- Who do we see to ensure that our teeth are straight and attractive? (Orthodontist)

English

3 UBINIG

The organization that helped Suriya is UBINIG. It is very important because it helps poor farmers make the most of the little land they have. Farmers who can grow crops well without chemicals make more money, because they don't have to buy the chemicals. And by not using chemicals, the farmers are looking after the environment: their soil is in better condition, there are more fish in the ponds and streams, and more wild plants grow, some of which they make medicines from. Ask the children to think about how Suriya farmed before and after UBINIG came to her village, and to write down how the results of the two ways of farming affected Suriya and the environment. Which way of farming was better? Why?

Science

4 Our environment

In groups, ask children to think how they could improve their school or local environment. For example, reduce litter in the school grounds, buy a composter for the school, or plant a nature garden. Make sure that they think about all the different experts they might have to ask for help.

Science, Citizenship

5. Local knowledge

Ask children, working in groups, to design an internet site or leaflet to show their expertise in an area of local knowledge. What would people coming from outside the area need to know? Ask the groups to pool their local knowledge (which they might well take for granted) to see how much specialist information they possess.

Art and design, English, Citizenship

REAL LIFE MAGIC

Suitable for KS2

Aims

To offer an image of hope, and of good triumphing over evil.

Preparation and materials

- Although it is not essential, this assembly will greatly benefit from a magic trick or illusion at the beginning. It may be that you, a member of staff or a pupil can perform a trick. You're looking for one with, if possible, a high visual impact that will come across in the assembly hall. There are plenty of simple tricks you can use without special equipment, either in books or on internet sites such as <www.kidzone.ws/>.
- You will need a bike (or large picture of one) and a picture of a gun (or a toy gun).
- Read through Sousa Manuel Goao's story in advance or prepare one or more children to read it.

Assembly

1. If you have one, perform your magic trick. If you don't have a trick, talk about magic and illusions and the sense of amazement and wonder they create.
2. Go on to mention the great staples of stage illusions – sawing someone in half; making someone levitate (float in the air); making people and things appear and disappear; turning something into something else; producing things out of seemingly impossible places, such as a rabbit out of a hat or an endless stream of silk cloths from a small box.
3. Talk about 'real life magic': that wonderful feeling when something actually happens that you had thought was impossible. Give some examples: you get picked for a

sports team, which a few months ago had seemed impossible; someone is ill and then, amazingly and against the odds, they get better; something you've been dreading and worrying about, like a test, turns out to be good – you even enjoy it! These are 'real life magic'; not tricks but events that give you the same feeling of surprise and wonder that a good trick does.

4. Explain that you have an example of real life magic that is so amazing that it sounds like a magic trick! The magic turns this (show gun/picture), into this (show bike/picture).

How is it done? In the Republic of Mozambique, a country in south-eastern Africa, an organization called the Christian Council of Mozambique swaps guns that are left over from the country's civil war (fighting among themselves) for useful things like a plough, a bike or a sewing machine. This is real life magic – they take weapons that did so much harm to the country and, hey presto, they turn them into useful things that help to build a better country for everyone.

5. But the magic doesn't stop there. Just like the best magic tricks that have an extra surprise at the end to make the audience gasp and applaud, the guns are given to artists who make them into works of art – sometimes they even make chairs and tables out of them. Read or ask the rehearsed children to read Sousa Manuel Goao's story.

My name is Sousa Manuel Goao. I live in a small village in Mozambique. When I was 23 years old I was kidnapped at gunpoint by anti-government rebel soldiers. I found myself with other young men that had been kidnapped. We were all forced to march for 150 miles – with no shoes!

After days of marching we finally arrived at a training camp in the middle of nowhere. We learnt how to survive. We also learnt how to raid farms and attack other people. We took whatever we wanted. We also kidnapped men to train as soldiers, just as we had been taken. We did not think about who we were killing – soldiers, men, women or children. It didn't matter.

Then, after a while, the rebel army that kidnapped me made an agreement with the government. So we stopped fighting and the government asked us to hand in our weapons. But we hid many of them. We needed to survive, so we kept the guns to help us get food and money.

Then I heard about the Christian Council of Mozambique. It was offering to give people tools, like ploughs and sewing machines, in return for their guns. I was hopeful. I wanted to stop running. I wanted to stop attacking people. So I nervously took in some guns. And I was amazed at what happened: I was treated with respect. The people at the Council gave me a sewing machine – no questions asked. Now I had a chance to earn a living!

Since then, I've given up more guns and in return I've had two more sewing machines. Now I work with my brother and my uncle and we make clothes to sell at the local market. I am so happy now there is peace in my life.

6. You could end by saying something like: I think we should show our appreciation for the brilliant real life magicians of Mozambique – cue applause!

 ## Time for reflection

Some magic is clever and amazes us with its fantastic tricks and illusions. So we ask: how did they do that?
Some magic is more everyday; we know how it happens but it still amazes and delights us. So we feel surprise and wonder.
And some magic seems to be both, like turning guns into bikes and making sculpture too!
What kind of magic can you do today? Who can you surprise and amaze?

 ## Prayer

Dear God,
Please help us to make magic in our daily lives
to surprise and amaze people with great new ideas,
just as the people of Mozambique did when they turned guns
into useful things and exciting art,
and to do small magic by being helpful, perhaps when people
least expect it.
Amen.

Class activities

1 Magic show

Can you stage a class magic show, like an extended version of the assembly? Use a variety of tricks with a development interpretation, such as:

- Making money disappear – how poorer countries struggle to have enough money for the basics of life.
- Card tricks – some countries have **diamonds** and others can't find them no matter how hard they dig with their **spades**; but we can all **club** together and have open **hearts** to the problems of others.
- Memory tricks – let's always remember that we live in a global village where we need to care for each other.

2 Peacemaker quiz

Talk about the real life magic of turning guns into art. Stress that this is an example of peacemaking: where people actively work to bring peace to their lives and the lives of others. Talk about peacemaking in school and at home. How can the children become peacemakers in their everyday life? Use the peacemaker quiz worksheet (page 96) to aid discussion.

PSHE, Citizenship

3 Guns into art

Can the children create images of works of art that rework symbols of war into expressions of peace? Some examples might be park benches made out of old missiles; plant pots made out of stacked guns; cartridge cases that become board game counters.

Art and design

4 Story

Write a short story called 'The Peacemaker'. It can be about any situation where one person's attitude and ideas help to bring peace. For example, a peacemaker at school who helps enemies to become friends; a peacemaker at home who helps to sort out an argument fairly; an artist in Mozambique who turns guns into artworks.

English

Peacemaker quiz

1 You are riding your bike on the pavement. As you turn a corner you nearly hit a woman. She shouts at you, saying that you are stupid and that she's going to tell the police about you. Do you:

   (a) Get upset and start to cry so much that you can hardly say sorry?
   (b) Wait for her to calm down and then say that you're sorry?
   (c) Shout back at her telling her that it was her fault for getting in your way?

2 You and a friend are arguing because one of you is lying. You know it isn't you. Do you:

   (a) Tell everyone about the argument and say that your friend is a liar?
   (b) Go to your friend and ask if you can sort things out because she's really important to you?
   (c) Ignore your friend and get all your other friends to ignore her as well to show her what you think of liars?

3 You are playing a game in the playground and someone trips you up. You're not sure if they did it on purpose or not. Do you:

   (a) Run and tell the teacher so that the person who tripped you up will get into trouble?
   (b) Stand up, brush yourself down and get on with your game?
   (c) Wait until the person who tripped you up comes near you and trip them up?

4 You are walking home from school with your friend. Suddenly someone from another school starts to shout and throw stones at you. One of the stones just misses your friend. Do you:

   (a) Run home tearfully?
   (b) Check that your friend is OK and then go back to school to tell your teacher about what happened?
   (c) Shout back at the person and throw stones at them?

Were your answers mainly (a), (b) or (c)? Count up how many you got of each letter and look at the bottom of the page to see what this says about you!

Answers

Mainly (a): You really don't like annoying people. Sometimes you need to take more responsibility for peacemaking rather than asking someone else to sort things out for you.

Mainly (b): You always try hard to be a peacemaker. You admit when you are wrong.

Mainly (c): You are not a good peacemaker. You only think of your own feelings.

Section 3
Children

HELPING OTHERS

Suitable for Whole School

 ### Aims

To explore the idea of children helping other children and their community, with a focus on a hygiene and a learning project in India.

 ### Preparation and materials

- Before the assembly get some children to paint well-known signs on large pieces of card: for example, a red traffic light, the symbol for motorway services, a no-smoking sign. Ask the children to hold up the signs during an assembly.
- Create two large signs: one that could mean 'clean drinking water', such as a glass of water with a tick or a smiley face next to it; and one that could mean 'dirty water: don't drink', such as a glass of water with an X or sad face next to it.
- Create a large sign that shows a happy face.
- Optional: Sign or board display showing 'The Ashish Gram Rachna Trust near Narayangaon'.

 ### Assembly

1. Arrange the children who have painted the signs in a line in front of the assembly with their cards face down. They should show their signs one by one. Ask the assembled children to tell you the meaning of the signs or symbols, using the following questions:

   - What does the sign or symbol mean?
   - How do you know? What tells you?
   - Where might you see this sign or symbol?
   - Why don't we use words to explain?

98

Why don't road signs say: 'Please keep your speed below 30 miles an hour, because this is a busy/dangerous road, thank you'? We use pictures to send a message because then everyone can understand it quickly without having to (a) understand the language (why might this be important?); (b) read (why might this be important?).

2. Are there signs that might save our lives? The red traffic light would stop your car being hit by others going across the junction. Can the children think of other examples, such as 'stay in your car' at a safari park, 'poison' on bottles, and so on? Who puts these signs up? (Adults!)

3. It's not just in this country today that we use such signs. The Ancient Egyptians used signs and symbols in their writing; we know them as hieroglyphics. And in a village called Narayangaon in central India, signs and symbols are saving lives – but this time it's the children that are using them.

   Show the children the sign that means clean or drinking water. Ask them what they think it means. Show the sign that means dirty water. What do they think this one means?

   Explain that a local organization wants to help people in the village live more healthy lives. There are no taps in the village and water has to be pumped from a well; and sometimes this water is not safe to drink. They have trained a number of children to go from house to house showing, through signs, whether or not the drinking water is safe to use that day; and the children have learnt how to test the purity of the well water.

   Imagine what could happen to people if they drank impure water or cooked with it. They would become ill and could even die. These children are saving lives.

4. Optional: Explain that as well as their work with the signs, some of the older children are helping the younger ones to learn. Read Jyoti's story.

Jyoti is 13. She lives with her parents and brothers in a village in Maharastra State, central India. She is still at primary school. The nearest secondary school is 5km away. But Jyoti wants to go to secondary school because she wants to be a doctor. Her mother wants her to be a teacher.

For Jyoti is a teacher already. Every evening she educates three younger girls in the village – Arachana, Savita and Vandana. She has been trained to teach basic reading, writing and maths. She wants to help others. She says: 'What I am learning, other children should know. No one should fool them.'

Savita is her keenest pupil. Savita is ten and has never been to school because she has to look after her three younger brothers. She says: 'I learn everything from Jyoti. I know numbers and the alphabet.'

Jyoti's mother is proud that her daughter is teaching. 'It is good for her and I am seeing a good change in her,' she says.

Savita's mother works as a day labourer to support her family. She does not want her only daughter to go to school just yet, but she lets her go to Jyoti's evening classes. 'I am happy that Savita is getting an education,' she says.

These children are being supported by the Ashish Gram Rachna Trust, an organization that trains people like Jyoti because it believes that children as well as adults can help their communities. Part of its work is persuading parents to send their children to school. It also trains children in health education, so they can tell families in their villages when the water is not safe to drink. The children discuss plans at the children's council (*bal panchayat*). There are councils in more than 30 villages, each with over 100 young members. Jyoti and her pupils are keen members of their children's council.

Savita's name means 'to do something good'. This story from India shows how children can do good things for others.

5. Optional: In the Bible it says that Jesus recognized how important children were, and said that they had a part to play in his kingdom.

Jesus said, 'Let the little children come to me. Don't stop them. The kingdom of God belongs to people who are like these little children. I tell you the truth. You must accept the kingdom of God as a little child accepts things, or you will never enter it.' (Mark 10.14–15, ICB)

6. Sum up by saying that in India, people recognize that children have an important role to play in helping other children and other people in their communities. What could *we* do in school, at home and in our neighbourhood?

 ## Time for reflection

We've been thinking about signs and symbols today. Take a look at this one (show the happy face).
What can you do to make this happen for those about you today?
What can children do to make the world a better place?

 ## Prayer

Dear God,
Help us to help each other, whether adults or children.
Thank you that we each have a special place in the world
and can all contribute to making the lives of others happier.
Amen.

 ## Class activities

1 Staying healthy

Jyoti and her friends in India are teaching people in their village how to be healthy. Discuss with the children the importance of washing their hands. Why do we wash our hands before we eat, or after using the toilet? What might happen if we don't wash our hands? At what other times is it important to wash our hands? After handling pets, helping in the garden, or painting.

Ask the children to devise a 'cartoon-style' sequence of pictures depicting the consequences of not washing their hands. Distilling a message to a series of pictures is a good skill to learn for literacy. Children who finish quickly could create sequences of pictures on other health issues, such as drinking clean water. Encourage a simple and clear graphical style rather than a complex one. You might insist, for example, on black and white line drawings, or a 'spot colour' approach with a sparing use of a single colour to create impact.

Art and design, PSHE, Citizenship

2 Signs and symbols

Make a collage of signs and symbols: collected, photographed or cut out of magazines. The children could bring some from home. What do the signs mean? Where are they found? Are they directed at children or at adults?

Ask the children what signs they could make to help people keep the rules in school. Ask them to suggest things that everybody needs to do to make school a happier place, such as tidying up litter, not bullying, and helping one another. This will contribute to a sense of citizenship and is particularly effective if children think of the issues themselves. Ask the children to create a sign that would remind others of one of these rules or principles, and display these in the classroom or around the school.

Art and design, PSHE, Citizenship

3 Teaching others

Pair your class up with a younger or older class and allow the older children to listen to the younger children read. Ask each older child to teach a new word to their younger partner, tell them a new story or teach them a new times table. Remind the children that Jyoti is only three years older than Savita, and yet she is teaching her language and number skills. Perhaps children could talk for a minute on a favourite hobby or explain how something works. They will see that it is difficult to teach others and that it requires patience and thought.

You could also try some role reversal where the younger children explain to the older ones what they have been doing in school that day.

Citizenship, PSHE

4 Story

Write a story called 'The day that changed my life'. Take your inspiration from the opportunities to learn that children in India now have as they learn from other children. Your story could be about an Indian child learning to write, who then becomes a writer or an actor or a leader of their country. It could be about someone in this country who learns something in history or maths, or any school subject, that makes a big difference to their life.

English

OPEN AIR SCHOOL

Suitable for Whole School

 Aims

To consider the importance of education and to value things that we often take for granted.

 Preparation and materials

- Prepare two people, preferably children, to read the interview.

 Assembly

1. Using your most serious voice, say that you have received an urgent communication from the government which must be read out to all schools at exactly (refer to watch and, perhaps pausing for dramatic effect, announce the current time). Open an official-looking envelope and read the following:

   > The government values education very highly and we are going to put more money into teaching maths and English. Unfortunately we don't have any more money so we have come up with a cunning plan. Starting today, all school buildings will be sold and all teaching will take place outside. This will be wonderful in the summer as children read and do their maths under shady trees. This will be wonderful in the autumn as children can see the wonders of nature and catch falling leaves for exercise. This will be wonderful in the winter as children will freeze up and stop being such a nuisance.

   Stop at this point. Either rip up the paper, throwing it away in disgust; or say 'Interesting' and slip it into your pocket!

2. Apologize for tricking the children but say that you wanted to make a point. Ask them what advantages they think there would be in having school outside (benefits of fresh air, plenty of space, chance to study nature at first hand); and the disadvantages (not hard to imagine given the climate!).

3. Introduce the interview with Mayna Sogheri from Afghanistan. She contracted malaria (a serious and life-threatening disease) because school lessons used to take place in the open air. With the help of local people and international charities, a school has now been built where children can attend classes in far better conditions.

Interviewer: Mayna, do you go to school?

Mayna: I am 15 and in the fifth class.

Interviewer: Do you remember school lessons when they took place under the trees before the school was built?

Mayna: I can remember there were lots of mosquitoes that would bite us all over and some girls would get malaria. I got malaria and had to go to the hospital.

Interviewer: What symptoms did you have?

Mayna: I was shaking, I had fever, and I was very hot. I was sick for about two weeks, trembling all the time.

Interviewer: How is the school now?

Mayna: It is much better now that we have a school building. When we had school in the open air we had to sit in the dust but in the school we have chairs and a water tap nearby. If we wanted to go to the toilet before we had to go all the way home and come back, but now there are toilets in the school.

Interviewer: Do you enjoy school?

Mayna: I really like school and enjoy all the subjects. My favourites are theology, Qur'an, Dari, geometry and maths. I don't like art, though, because it's very difficult and I have to really concentrate.

4. Explain that 'theology' is learning about religion, the Qur'an is Islam's holy book, and Dari is Mayna's language. Point out that although she is older, Mayna is very much like all of you. She has her favourite subjects at school and others which she doesn't like so much! But perhaps the most important thing to think about is not what she learns at school but that she now has a school building to go to. Before this she might have died from disease! Many children around the world don't have any schooling and many don't have school buildings either.

Time for reflection

Think about Mayna's life before the school was built: 'I was shaking, I had fever, and I was very hot. I was sick for about two weeks, trembling all the time.'
And after: 'It is much better now that we have a school building. I really like school and enjoy all the subjects.'

Prayer

Dear God,
Thank you that Mayna now has a school because of the hard work of many people.
Thank you for our school building and all the things that we have in it.
And thank you for all the people who study and work in it.
Amen.

Class activities

1 Open air school
Talk further about schooling in the open air and ask the children to come up with ideas for lessons that could be taught well outside.

English

2 **Mayna's letter**
Imagine that Mayna has just recovered from malaria and is
well enough to attend her first day at the new school. Write a
letter, as if from Mayna, to someone in the UK, telling about
her first day at the new school.

English

3 **Design**
In groups, ask children to design their own school buildings,
allowing for indoor and outdoor teaching and activities.

Design

4 **Improvisation**
In pairs or small groups, ask children to improvise a scene in
which villagers in Afghanistan try to persuade someone from
the government to build a school, giving as many reasons as
possible.

Drama

COMMUNITY OF HOPE

Suitable for KS2

Aims

To raise an awareness of children who have lost parents to diseases and how they can be helped, and to explore the idea that we all belong to and need some kind of community.

Preparation and materials

- This assembly is based on the experiences of children whose parents have died, in this case due to HIV-related illnesses, but it can apply equally to any disease or natural disaster. Sensitivity will be needed towards children who have suffered a recent bereavement.
- The sketch will need some rehearsal with a class or year group. Or you could tell the story as part of the assembly instead.
- You will need three gym hoops of different colours and a long rope or ribbon, or chalk.
- Optional: Whiteboard, OHP or flipchart.

Assembly

1. Start by asking the children what they think a community is. Work towards a simple definition, such as 'a group of people who feel they belong together'. Ask the children what community they are in at the moment (i.e. the name of the school). Invite them to suggest other communities they belong to, such as families, Brownies, Cubs, any other clubs.
2. Invite some volunteers (four to six depending on the size of your hoops!) to the front and say: 'If you belong to the community of (your school name) stand in the red hoop.' Hopefully they will all stand in the red hoop. Now say: 'If

you belong to the community of X (choose a sub-group that two or three will belong to, like a particular class), stand in the blue hoop.' Some children will go from the red hoop into the blue one.

Ask those that have moved: 'Aren't you in the school community any more? Shouldn't you be in both at the same time? How can we show that?'

Devise a way of showing a big circle to represent the school into which you can put the smaller circle representing the class or sub-group. Ways of achieving this include:

- Lay a rope or ribbon in a large circle on the floor.
- Draw a chalk line on the floor.
- Say that the whole space represents the school.
- Move from a practical to a drawn representation using a whiteboard, OHP or flipchart.

3. Now say to the volunteers: 'If you belong to the community of the whole world stand in the green hoop.' If any of them moved to the green hoop, ask them: 'Aren't you in at least one of these other communities as well?'

Explain that we need an even bigger hoop – a world-sized hoop – to make a set of everyone. How can we show this? Take the children's suggestions. One good way would be to say that the whole assembly hall represents the community of the world, which contains all the sub-groups including the school and the class. You could illustrate this by hanging a large sheet of paper showing the words 'The Whole World' in a prominent position or by making a large banner which a group of children can hold.

Summarize by explaining that we all belong to different communities and to the world community at the same time. It's not always easy to remember that we are all in the world hoop and there is enough room and enough resources for all of us in there.

4. Introduce the sketch and those taking part.

Leader: This is about some children who belong to one small community in Kenya in east Africa.

A group of three children move to sit in a hoop. Three other children, Gatura, Makena and Zuri, stand behind them.

Child 1:   I'm Gatura.
Child 2:   I'm Makena.
Child 3:   I'm Zuri.
Leader: They play together (*Gatura, Makena and Zuri do a clapping game*).
            They learn together (*raise hands as if in a classroom*).
            They pray together (*bow heads*).
            They eat together (*pass around an imaginary bowl*).
            They are part of one small community – and are proud of it! (*put arms around each other's shoulders*).

            Gatura, Makena and Zuri have each lost one or both of their parents because of a serious illness. They are very sad not to live with their parents but they belong to a very special community – the Forty Families Project. This project takes care of their needs and each child is given a guardian to look after them.

A child from the hoop group puts their arm around Gatura.

            Each child's school fees are paid and they get a new school uniform.

A child from the hoop group mimes doing up Makena's tie.

            Their guardians learn how to farm their land well, so there is plenty of food, and they are given money to start a little business.

A child from the hoop group and Zuri mime working on the land.

            They all feel included in this strong community of loving people. Although they are far away from here, they are part of the world community – and you are too.

5. Explain that losing a parent is about the worst thing that can happen to anyone, but that a loving and caring community can help even in this terrible situation.

 ## Time for reflection

Let's think for a moment about children all over the world who have lost their parents to HIV-related illnesses, malaria, cancer and other terrible diseases.

Let's think about how fortunate we are and how we are all part of communities: family, school, perhaps clubs, societies or teams, perhaps churches or mosques, temples or synagogues, our country and even the world. We are part of the same world community as the children we've been hearing about today.

 ## Prayer

Let's pray for children like Gatura, Makena and Zuri and the adults who care for them.

We think of children all over the world whose parents have died,

and thank God that communities can provide hope even in those terrible situations.

Amen.

 ## Class activities

1 Belonging to communities

Ask the children to think about the groups that they belong to: school, family, Brownies or Cubs, faith group, the world. Then invite them to move physically into various sets, for instance those who go to Brownies or Cubs, those in a sports club. Encourage them to see that we are all part of many overlapping communities.

List the sets discussed and ask children to draw Venn diagrams showing which sets they are in. Discuss how to show overlapping sets.

Talk about being a member of a community: caring for and belonging to each other; obeying the rules of the group.

PSHE, Maths, Citizenship

2 William's story

Read William's story below and discuss with the children the differences between his life and theirs. What does Josephine do for William and the other children? How does she make William feel that 'this is where I belong'?

My name is William. I am 11 and I go to Nyangoma school in Bondo district in Kenya. Let me tell you about my life.

In many ways I think it is just like yours. I like going to primary school each day, although it is quite a long walk through the bush. I love playing football with my best friend Josiah and winning races against my sisters, Risper who is 10 and Synthia who is 8. On Sundays it's fun to go to our church to sing songs.

I know our lives are also different from yours. I live in a very different kind of house from you. It is my job to look after our cows and to collect water from the river.

We live with my grandparents because our mum and dad died when I was very little. It makes me feel sad sometimes.

Because I don't have any parents I have a guardian called Josephine. She visits us every day and makes sure that we have everything we need. She pays for us to go to school and helps us with our homework. She always listens to our problems. We are very grateful for her. She plays lots of games with us too.

Sometimes, in the evening, we eat *ugali* – a stiff porridge made from maize – with fish and vegetables, and Josephine tells stories about her life and the history of our community. Josephine is always there for me. She makes me feel that this is where I belong.

PSHE, Citizenship

3 The Forty Families community

Discuss what the orphans need to feel part of a community. Write a list on the board of the suggested answers, such as love, friends, a home, good health.

Make a class collage or painting, showing what it means to be part of this special community. Increase the children's cooperation by asking pairs to work together to produce

 # A day in the life...

William, Risper and Synthia Okello live in Kenya. As their mother and father are dead, their guardian, Josephine, looks after them. They live on their grandmother's farm. Below is an average day for William. In the space, write what you would be doing at the same time on an average day.

Night time **We sleep on the floor at our grandmother's house.**

6 o'clock **We wake up and have tea for breakfast.**

7 o'clock **It takes nearly an hour to walk to school!**

8 o'clock to midday **School-time! My favourite subject is maths. Risper and Synthia love Kiswahili, our second language. We all love school.**

1 o'clock **We have lunch at home. We eat** *ugali* **(like a thick porridge) and fish.**

2 o'clock to 4 o'clock **It's school again for Risper and me. Synthia stays at home and does her chores. She washes the dishes and sweeps up.**

5 o'clock **We get home. Often we stay in our school uniforms because we don't have other clothes.**

6 o'clock **It's time to do our homework. Our guardian, Josephine, often helps us out.**

7 o'clock **We have supper with our grandparents. It's usually** *ugali***, fish from the lake and vegetables again.**

8 o'clock **We all have some time to play. Synthia likes to do French-skipping with her friends. Sometimes we have running races together.**

9 o'clock or even later! **Bed-time!**

mini-scenes for a class collage. Use the story of William to explore why his guardian is so special.

Encourage your children to think of people in their community who act like guardians by caring for them, being there when they are needed, such as parents, teachers, grandparents. Invite children to devise an award and certificate for 'special people in our lives' and to nominate someone for the award.

PSHE, Citizenship, Art and design

4 Worksheet

Copy the 'A day in the life ... ' worksheet (page 113) for the children and ask them to fill in the column on the right-hand side. What are the similarities and what are the differences between their lives and those of William, Risper and Synthia?

PSHE, Citizenship

5 Circle time

Knowing that you are listened to and respected is an important element in feeling part of a community. Hold a circle time session, in which children take it in turns to say one thing that they liked about this subject and one thing they didn't. Give some time for reflection and write everyone's comments on a big piece of paper for display.

PSHE

LOSING EVERYTHING –
AND STILL THERE'S HOPE

Suitable for KS2

 Aims

To show how people who face terrible disaster can, with the help of others, begin to rebuild their lives.

 Preparation and materials

- You will need a wig, a pair of glasses, a set of joke teeth (or use 'gum-teeth' sweets).
- A cuddly toy or a diary (to represent favourite possessions).
- A school tie or T-shirt (to represent your school).
- A set of keys (to represent your house).
- Three volunteers – one to narrate Sylvia's story, one to read what she says and one to hold/wear the props.
- A Bible, if you are reading Psalm 100.

 Assembly

1. Ask if anyone has heard this expression: You don't know what you've got till it's gone. What do they think it means? That sometimes we only recognize the value of something when we no longer have it. Ask for examples, such as something you swapped or sold and then wished you hadn't, or a friend who moved away and you didn't realize how much you would miss them.
2. Explain that you have brought a few things with you today to illustrate that we often don't realize how important things are until we no longer have them. Ask one of your volunteers to come to the front and put the different items on or hold them up as you say the following. This works particularly well if

the volunteer is a teacher with not much hair who is game for a laugh!

Do you ever feel grateful for your hair or your eyesight or even your teeth? (Volunteer puts on wig, glasses and teeth.) Are you pleased to be able to come to school? (Puts on school tie or T-shirt.) Think about your favourite possessions. How often do we remember to be grateful for them? (Give volunteer a cuddly toy or diary.) I wonder if you remember to be thankful for your house, or do you wish it was bigger or newer? (Give volunteer your keys.)

3. Some of us might lose our hair (remove wig), or our teeth (take teeth back), or our eyesight might get worse (remove glasses), but often that doesn't happen until we're a bit older. At that stage, we'll probably miss these things and wish we had them back!

Hopefully, we'll never have to lose our school (remove tie/T-shirt), or our possessions (take toy/diary back) or homes (take keys).

Leave the items out where the pupils can see them.

4. Explain that all around the world people lose these things for different reasons. This is the story of someone who lost everything.

Eleven-year-old Sylvia and her family live in Sri Lanka, an island off the south-east coast of India. Until Christmas 2004, their house was beside the sea. But when the Indian Ocean tsunami (giant wave) hit the island, their home was washed away by the water. Huge waves carried Sylvia out to sea. She managed to cling to a log and held on for more than 24 hours until an army helicopter flying overhead spotted and rescued her. Sadly, her nine-year-old brother and her best friend weren't so lucky; they both died.

A year later, life still wasn't back to normal for Sylvia. She lived in a special camp with her mum, dad and older sister and lots of other families who also had lost their homes and loved ones. She said at the time: 'Life is a little better now but whenever I hear the sound of the waves, I start to remember what happened on that day. Or if I hear the sound of pouring rain I remember and it makes me very frightened. It is difficult to live here in the camp. People often start rumours that a tsunami is coming. I would feel safer far away.'

People just like you all over the world were shocked by what happened in 2004 and acted quickly to raise as much money as they could to give to charities that would help people affected by the tsunami. These charities work with local organizations and one of these charities, called Thadaham, helped children like Sylvia by talking and playing with them; getting them to do the 'normal' things that they did before the tsunami.

That was all a few years ago but the local organizations have not forgotten Sylvia and the other people who lost everything in the tsunami, including loved ones. It is very hard to start again as Sylvia has done, but, with the help of other people and gifts from around the world, it is possible; there is hope.

5. You could read Psalm 100. Explain that the passage reminds us to be grateful for everything we have.

 ## Time for reflection

Even though the tsunami happened a while ago, many people are still affected by it; those who lost loved ones still miss them. For most of us, it's hard to imagine how that might feel. Spend a few moments thinking about what you've heard today about people losing so much, but still finding the hope and help they need to start again.

 ## Prayer

Ask the children to put the fingertips of each hand together in the shape of a roof.

> From the comfort of our homes, let us pray for those whose homes have been destroyed.

Ask the children to point their joined fingertips forward in the shape of the bow (front) of a boat.

From the safety of our school, let us pray for those who fish and work on the sea.

Ask the children to cross their arms over their chests.

From hearts full of sadness, in a moment of quiet, let us pray for those who have suddenly lost family members or friends.

Amen.

Class activities

1 Looking at disasters

Ask the children what they think a disaster is. When have they heard someone say, 'It's a disaster!'? What were they referring to? Do people sometimes use the phrase too lightly? As a class, decide what your definition of a disaster is.

Give out copies of the 'What is a disaster?' worksheet (page 119) and ask the class to work in small groups to complete it. Alternatively, you could print each element of the worksheet on to bigger pieces of paper and ask members of the class to stand in a line holding a sheet each. As a class you then decide what order they should be in (biggest to smallest – see worksheet).

PSHE

2 Research

Working in pairs, children can research recent disasters with the aim of finding out the following.

- What happened?
- How were people affected?
- How did people around the world respond?
- What efforts are being made to help the people affected start again?
- What could we do to help?

They can present their findings as a report to the class, a written report or an audio podcast.

Research skills, English

What is a disaster?

Write your definition of a disaster here:

_____

_____

Which of these things do you think is the worst disaster? Number them in order of how big a disaster you think they are with number 1 being the biggest and number 8 being the smallest.

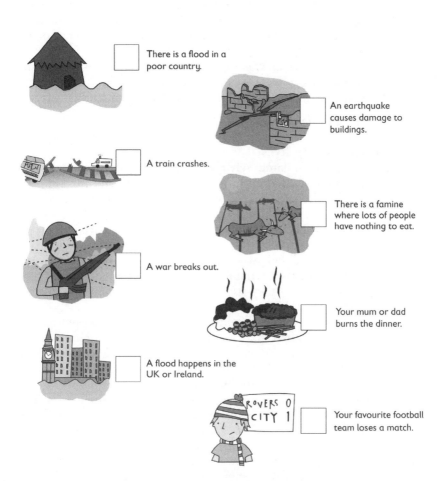

There is a flood in a poor country.

An earthquake causes damage to buildings.

A train crashes.

There is a famine where lots of people have nothing to eat.

A war breaks out.

Your mum or dad burns the dinner.

A flood happens in the UK or Ireland.

Your favourite football team loses a match.

3 Thoughts and feelings

Reread Sylvia's story. Then split the class into small groups and give each group a large sheet of paper. Ask them to draw an outline of a person to represent Sylvia. Round the outside of Sylvia they should write down everything that happened to her and all the things she lost. Inside the outline, they should write down how they think Sylvia might have felt. Then ask them to draw a line from things on the outside to the feeling on the inside they think goes best with it. They can use a feeling more than once. Alternatively you could do this as a whole class activity using a very large sheet of paper and drawing round a child lying on the floor.

When Sylvia was visited a year after the tsunami, she seemed happier. Discuss with the children whether that surprises them and why they think she seemed this way.

Art and design, PSHE

4 Rebuilding lives

Since the tsunami, Sylvia's life has been very different from the lives of children in places like the UK and Ireland. Ask the children to write down what they do during a normal week. They could keep a diary for a week of all the things they do. They should remember to include what they do after school and at the weekend.

Much of their week will be taken up with school. Ask them what they would do each day if they couldn't go to school. Would they still do these things if they were feeling sad or frightened?

Discuss with the children if they think it's important that everyday things like school and play were organized for Sylvia and the other children. Why? Is it a good use of the money raised? Why? Or is it more important for Sylvia to have a new home and possessions?

Ask the class to list what was back to normal in Sylvia's life a year after the tsunami and what wasn't. From the list of things that are not back to normal, identify which can be sorted out and which may never be normal for Sylvia.

Imagine that you are organizing children's activities at a camp for disaster victims. Write out the daily timetable.

PSHE, English

5 Thinking about disasters

Ask the class to reflect on what they have learnt about the tsunami and other disasters. Remind them that they have learnt how it affected people physically and emotionally as well as what actually happened. You could use the activity on the worksheet (page 119) to help children understand that these effects might be very different in a rich country.

PSHE, Citizenship

ADA'S SONGS

Suitable for KS1

 Aims

To suggest that children living far away are very much like children in the UK but that sometimes their lives are much harder.

 Preparation and materials

- You might like to prepare one or more children to read Ada's words, or you can do this yourself.
- The assembly includes a simple song to the tune of 'Here we go round the mulberry bush', which can be sung easily accompanied or unaccompanied.

 Assembly

1. Talk to the children about their mornings on school days: What time do they get up? What do they have for breakfast? How do they come to school? What time do they arrive at school? What do they do when they get there?
2. Tell the children about Ada, who lives in Mali in western Africa. How much you explain about the country will depend on the children's knowledge: some may have come from African countries or have visited relatives, others may have little idea of the continent. Ensure that the children understand that Mali is a long way from the UK and that many people there are farmers without much money.

   Ada is six years old and she goes to school when she can, but she also has to help with the harvest: helping to collect the crops (plants) from the field when they have fully grown. Point out that Ada's life might seem very different from the children's lives, but listen to the words of this song that she sings about her mother:

My mother, I love my mother, who took care of me when
   I was a baby.
When I was crying she comforted me.
When I was hungry she gave me food.
She taught me how to speak, step by step from one word
   to one sentence.
I will love my mother all my life and I will do everything I
   can to make her happy.

So perhaps she's not so different from us after all!

3. Explain that in a moment you're going to teach the children
   another song that Ada sings, but to understand it you need to
   tell them about a problem that Ada and everyone in Mali
   faces: swarms of locusts. Thousands and thousands of these
   insects, like grasshoppers, try to eat the crops that Ada's
   family and friends have grown. Here's what Ada says about
   them:
   'I remember the locusts coming. We were in the fields at
   the time. People came and told us locusts were coming. We
   just stared at them. They sounded like a car motor, a
   prrrprrprr noise. They smelt like fresh fish, like when you've
   touched fish and then smell your hand.'
   If the people hear the locusts coming there is something
   they can do: they can make a big noise to frighten the insects
   off. Everyone rushes outside, shouting, banging drums or
   pots and pans – doing anything they can to make a loud
   noise. One time the swarm of locusts just missed them; they
   swerved away just in time because of the loud noise.

4. Optional: Play a game where the children make a *controlled*
   loud noise, such as clapping and calling out, 'Locusts be
   gone!' when you say the key word 'locust'; but only when
   you say that word. Ask everyone to look at you, then you
   very quietly whisper 'locust'. Then hold up your hand for
   silence. Do this a few times. You could throw in some
   wildcards to trick them, such as 'locomotive' or 'lowdown' or
   'loads of chocolate'. Before moving on, stress that this noisy
   game is now over!

5. Another thing that the people can do about locusts is to
   destroy the tiny eggs that locusts lay, whenever they find
   them. Ada likes doing this and she sings a song as she does it.

Here's an English version of it (to the tune of 'Here we go round the mulberry bush'):

> Here we are squashing locust eggs, locust eggs, locust eggs.
> Here we are squashing locust eggs, squash, squash, squash.

Teach the song and add some simple squashing actions.

6. End by saying that life is very hard for Ada and her family. She is often very hungry because the locusts have eaten their crops. Here's what she says:

'The hunger we are going through in our village is not because we haven't worked hard. It's because of locusts not laziness.'

 ## Time for reflection

Spend a few moments thinking about Ada and how different her life is from yours:
She has to work in the fields.
Sometimes she is very hungry but there is no food.
She has been very ill because of lack of food.

But Ada is just the same as you in lots of ways too:
She goes to school.
She loves her mother and father.
She likes to sing.

 ## Prayer

> Dear God,
> We pray for people like Ada and her family as they try to grow crops and beat the locusts.
> We pray for a fairer world, where everyone has enough to eat.
> **Amen.**

Class activities

1 Song

Practise Ada's locust song in class, developing new movements to go with the words.

Music

2 Choral speaking

Teach the words of this version of Ada's song about her mother:

> I love my mother.
> When I was a baby she cared for me.
> If I cry she comforts me.
> When I'm hungry she feeds me.
> She taught me how to speak.
> Step by step, word by word, sentence by sentence.
> I will love my mother all my life.
> And I will make her happy.

Rehearse this with different individuals or groups taking some lines, others said all together. You could present this in an assembly.

English

3 Writing

Teach the words 'Mali', 'Africa', 'Ada' and 'locust'. Can the children put them together in a sentence?

English

4 Collage

Create a class collage showing the people in Ada's village making a noise as the locusts descend on the crops. Fabric could be used for the villagers and the locusts could be made with lots of tiny dark dots, pointillist style.

Art

HOW MUCH IS A PERSON WORTH?

Suitable for KS2

 Aims

To think about the value of human life and the importance of education.

 Preparation and materials

- You will need six £1 coins (or the rough equivalent in local currency, such as €7 or US$10).
- A range of items each costing approximately £6 (€7), for example, a fancy box of chocolates, a pack of socks, cinema ticket, portion of meat.
- Prepare two volunteers to read Venkatamma's story: one narrates and the other reads Venkatamma's words. Alternatively, the story could be split between more readers.
- A Bible if you are reading Luke 12.6–7.

 Assembly

1. Ask the children what they could buy with £6 (€7). Value all sensible suggestions and if appropriate add some suggestions of your own to ensure that there is a shared concept of the value of £6 (€7).
2. Ask if a monetary value can be put on a person. Depending on the age of the children, encourage discussion about how people relate to monetary value, such as the cost of schooling, wages, how much a person spends on themselves, and the cost of healthcare. Draw the discussion towards the idea that people can't be 'priced' in the way that objects and services can – or can they?

3. Introduce Venkatamma's story:

> *Reader*: Venkatamma is 11 and goes to school in Andhra Pradesh in southern India. But until a short time ago she spent all day, every day, looking after ten buffaloes. It was hard work for a child. They weren't even her own family's buffaloes – they belonged to a farmer who Venkatamma had been sold to. And do you know how much her family got paid in return for selling her? £6 (€7). Not £6 (€7) a day, or even a week; just £6 (€7) in total. Her family didn't want to sell her, but they had no choice because they were so poor. Venkatamma says:
>
> *Venkatamma*: One day one of the buffaloes went into someone else's field and ruined some crops. The farmer was very angry and he beat me. I escaped by running away to my sister's home. I started crying and stopped eating. I kept saying, 'I want to go to school.' After three days, my sister brought me to the Bridge School.
>
> *Reader 1*: The Bridge School is run by an Indian organization supported by charities in the UK and Ireland. It is for children who haven't been to school before. Venkatamma has been at the school for about a year now and it has changed her life. She says:
>
> *Venkatamma*: I would like to go to university. I want to become something important like a teacher and feel that I am helping the community.

4. Remind the children that Venkatamma was sold for just £6 (€7) – which would only buy you a few music tracks or a cheap DVD. But thanks to charities here and local organizations in India, she's now going to school. Why do you think going to school is so important? Value the children's suggestions and get to the key points:

- Children can learn things that will help them to get a job.
- They can learn how to be more healthy and stay safe.
- They can help their community and their country to climb out of poverty.

Also take ideas that suggest that school may not be always popular. It doesn't always feel like a good thing and sometimes, like when you have to get up on a cold, dark school morning or be inside when the sun is shining, we can all think of other places we might like to be. But without education in this country we would be living in a society of poverty for most and extreme wealth for a few. Education is the way out of poverty and ignorance, and that's what we want for children across the world like Venkatamma.

More than 100 million children across the world don't get the chance to go to school. That's 100 million children like Venkatamma who either have to work instead of going to school, or have to stay at home because their parents can't afford to send them to school.

5. You could read Luke 12.6–7. Explain that Christians and members of other faiths believe that God cares for each one of us, and values us as worth a bit more than two pennies, or £6 (€7), or any sum of money you care to name!

 ## Time for reflection

How much are you worth?
Think of any sum of money you can – it won't be enough.
Think of the most expensive thing possible: a private plane, a private spacecraft, your own island, your own country, your own planet, your own universe ... But none of these things can think and feel and live and love like you can. You're priceless.

 ## Prayer

Dear God,
Thank you for caring for each of us.
We thank you that we are able to come to school without paying.

We think of Venkatamma and how she was sold for just £6
(€7).
We thank you for the work of charities that have made it
possible for her to go to school.
Help us to be grateful for our education and to do all we can to
make sure that the 100 million children around the world
who aren't in school at the moment will be very soon.
Amen.

 Class activities

1 £6 (€7) for a person
On pieces of A3 paper, ask the children to draw an outline of
a girl to represent Venkatamma. Give the class some mail-
order catalogues (or use the internet) and ask them to fill
Venkatamma's outline with items that cost approximately
£6 (€7). You could display the filled outlines alongside
Venkatamma's story as used in the assembly.

Art and design, PSHE, Citizenship

2 Why school?
Explain that Venkatamma's story is sad not just because she
was sold for £6 (€7), but also because she didn't get to go to
school until the local organization helped her. In pairs, ask
children to make a list of the advantages and disadvantages of
going to school. Can they see the benefits of education? Using
the advantages write a class acrostic or haiku-style poem.

PSHE, Citizenship, English

3 No choice
Remind the class of the previous activity and the importance
of education. Then ask them to imagine that they are
Venkatamma, looking after buffaloes day in, day out.
Explain that Venkatamma used to watch as other children
from the village went to school. Ask the children to write a
brief extract from Venkatamma's diary where she explains
how she feels and why she was desperate to go to school.

PSHE, Citizenship, English

4 If I ran the school ...

What do the children think is important to learn in school? Working in pairs, can they come up with a timetable for a week in a school that they run? What will be on the curriculum (what will children learn?), and how will the day be organized? How much holiday will there be each year? At the end of their schooling what will young people be able to do? If they were designing the school for Venkatamma – would anything be different?

English, PSHE, Citizenship

Section 4
War and peace

FAR FROM HOME

Suitable for Whole School

Aims

To help children understand why people become refugees and the reality of life for many who are forced to leave their homes.

Preparation and materials

- Rehearse the play in advance. You will need five pupils or members of staff for the parts of TV reporter, newsreader, Mrs Crabbit, her son Kyle, and Bumeh.
- Three readers for Bumeh's story.
- A coat and microphone (could be a dummy) for the TV reporter and a desk for the newsreader.
- Some music to play as the theme tune to the TV show. You could use 'Our House' by Madness.

Assembly

1. Start the assembly by asking whether any of the children have moved house recently. Were they happy to move? What do they miss from their old house?
2. Introduce the play by explaining that they're going to see a pilot for a new TV show. Play the theme music.

> *TV reporter:* Hello and welcome to *Moving On Up*, the show that brings you the best house moves, live and happening! Move up, move out, get rich quick with *Moving On Up*. And we begin today's show with the Crabbit family. They are moving from Sleepytown Drive to a new house in Greenwood Avenue. (*Turns towards Mrs Crabbit.*) So, Mrs Crabbit, why do you

want to move house? This looks like a good enough area for you to live in.

Mrs Crabbit: Well, Jeremy (or Jemima), we want to move to a bigger house so the children can each have their own room. Also I want a patio and decking out the back and my husband wants a double garage – we've only got one car but it looks good, don't you think? And then there's the kitchen, it's got …

TV reporter: (interrupting) Yes, but if I could just …

Mrs Crabbit: (interrupting) … simply got to have room for a triple fridge freezer with ice cube maker and MP3 player. So yes, I'll be sad to leave Sleepytown Drive, but I know it's the best thing to do.

TV reporter: Thank you. Mrs Crabbit's son Kyle is here with us too. What do you think about moving house, Kyle?

Kyle: I feel really sad about it. I don't think it's fair that we have to move. I want my own room, but I will miss seeing my friends every day and I don't care about the stupid kitchen.

Mrs Crabbit: Kyle! Wash your mouth out – that kitchen means a lot to me.

Newsreader: Although the Crabbits are moving to a new house, their son Kyle is very unhappy about it. Sometimes moving somewhere new can be an adventure; at other times it can be very sad. Sometimes it's both! But some people don't even have a choice about whether they move or not. *Moving On Up* brings you the story of Bumeh, a girl who was born in Burma but now lives in Thailand.

Reader 1: Bumeh is 11 years old and has four brothers and sisters. She lives on the Thai–Burmese border in a refugee camp but was born in Burma. Burma is a very beautiful country, but has had a lot of problems. It was once one of the richest countries in Asia, but is now ruled by a military government. For 50 years, the army has been fighting with different ethnic groups of people, including the Karenni, which Bumeh's family belongs to.

Five years ago, soldiers attacked Bumeh's village in the night and burnt down her family's house and barn. Her parents woke her and said that they had to leave the country as quickly as they could. Bumeh was very frightened. The family fled across the border into Thailand, where they now live in a bamboo hut in the refugee camp. It's not safe for them to go back to Burma. Bumeh's home in the camp is very simple, but it is really important to her. She knows what it feels like to lose her real home.

Newsreader: Bumeh isn't the only person to be in this situation. Today, millions of children around the world are refugees. Now let's hear the end of Bumeh's story.

Reader 2: A year after they arrived, Bumeh's mum died of malaria. Bumeh was very sad. It is hard for her dad to look after five children on his own. But the family have been helped with food and shelter by an organization called the Thailand Burma Border Consortium, which in turn was given money by a charity in the UK and Ireland. Life is still difficult. Every day Bumeh has to help her dad with the chores. She cooks, collects water and feeds the pigs. She goes to school, but her home doesn't have electricity so she does her homework in the evenings by oil lamp.

Reader 3: Bumeh says: 'I want to be a nurse when I grow up, and help those who are sick, especially because my mum died of malaria. I don't remember very much about my homeland, but I would like to go back some day, to see where I was born.'

Time for reflection

Let's think about the challenges that people face when they move to a new place. Think about how you could welcome someone who has moved near you.

All the major world faiths say that we should look after people who come to our country from other places. The Bible tells us that Jesus himself was a refugee when he was only two years old, and his family took him to Egypt to escape King Herod.

Think about what it was like for Bumeh when she had to leave her home. Let's be thankful that there are organizations helping Bumeh and her family.

 Prayer

Whatever faith we belong to, we are asked to welcome strangers and to care for those who have lost their home.

Sometimes we know what it is like to feel lost and lonely in a strange place.

> Dear God,
> Help us to be welcoming and kind to everyone, especially those who are in a new area or a new home, or even far from home.
> **Amen.**

 Class activities

1 My place

Our homes are very important to us, wherever they are. Ask your class to draw a picture of their home. Older children could do this as a floor plan. Ask the children to draw what happens in each room.

2 Home words

With the children, make a list of the words that home can represent. For example, comfort, security, fun, family, Christmas, Diwali. Ask them to choose their favourite words and write them around their home in their pictures.

Explain that Bumeh had a home that she loved too, but

she was forced to leave it. Read the whole of Bumeh's story to your class. Ask them to think about how they would feel if they were Bumeh. Write these thoughts in the form of a letter to Bumeh or a poem.

Art and design, PSHE, English

3 Pack your bags!

Print copies of the 'Pack your bags!' worksheet (page 137). Explain that Bumeh had only a few seconds to grab what she wanted to take with her when she left her home. Begin by making a list of all the types of things that the children have in their houses (using categories such as toys and furniture). Then ask them to answer these questions:

- What things would you want to take with you if you left in a hurry?
- What things would be practical to take?
- What things would you want to take because they were important to you?
- What things would be too heavy or not useful enough?

Tell the children that they have just three minutes to decide what they would take with them. Discuss the things they choose, then hand out the worksheets for them to draw and label their choices. Then ask them to share their decisions with the rest of the class. Ask the children to explain their reasons and to write about how they felt about having to make such choices.

PSHE, English

4 Into the unknown

Design the cover for a book based on Bumeh's experiences. Call the book 'Into the Unknown', or make up your own title. Also write the back cover copy. How will you make the book look and sound exciting and interesting so that readers will want to buy it?

English, Art and design

Pack your bags!

Name _____

You have three minutes to pack your bag and leave home. It's a tough choice – what will you take and what will you leave behind? Think about which things are most important to you and what will be most useful. Remember that you also have to carry your own bag!

Draw and label the things you decided on.

Now list your items and explain why you chose them...

I chose _____ because _____

_____

I chose _____ because _____

_____

I chose _____ because _____

_____

PEACE ON EARTH?

Suitable for KS2

 ### Aims

To help children reflect on the reality of war and the need for peace and conflict resolution.

 ### Preparation and materials

- Rehearse the readers for Eduardo's story in advance and practise the actions/sounds: hot sun, heavy rain, blowing dust, sitting on stones. The story is split between three readers but could easily be either expanded or read by just one or two children.
- If you are using this material at Christmas time, you might like to include a reading from Luke 2.8–15 with its message about peace on earth.

 ### Assembly

1. Explain that you are going to describe some situations and you'd like the children to make appropriate noises and actions (you might like to demonstrate!):

   - **hot sun** beating down on their heads (sheltering under hands, flapping hands in front of face, sighing)
   - **heavy rain** pouring down (fingertips drumming on floor to make rain sound, covering head with hands)
   - **dust** blowing in their faces (hands in front of face, swishing sound of dusty wind)
   - **sitting** on uncomfortable stones (fidgeting!).

2. Settle the children, allowing the fidgeting to end before you continue. Ask them to guess where they were – the place

where they had to put up with the sun, rain, dust and uncomfortable stones. Tell them they were at school!

Explain that the school had been vandalized by soldiers fighting a war so it couldn't be used. Ask the children to think of what they like about their school. Can they imagine having their lessons outside in the rain or sitting on stones instead of chairs?

3. Introduce Eduardo's story:

Reader 1: Eduardo is 13 years old. He lives in a small town in Angola, which is a country in southern Africa. For many years there was a civil war where groups in the country fought against each other. Thousands of families ran away from their homes to escape the fighting, and lots of people were killed or injured.

Reader 2: One day, soldiers attacked Eduardo's village. Eduardo and his family ran away and hid in the nearby mountains. Because they had to leave so quickly, they couldn't take much with them. All they had to eat was a type of porridge called *funge*. After the fighting in his village stopped, Eduardo and his family went back home. The soldiers had destroyed parts of the village, and the school was a ruin, with no roof, shutters or furniture. Eduardo and his friends had to sit on stones instead of chairs, and their lessons were often stopped by heavy rain or thick dust blowing.

Reader 1: A peace deal was signed in 2002 and later a local organization helped the villagers to build a new roof for the school and put shutters on the windows; they also gave the school desks and chairs. Now Eduardo and his friends don't get covered in dust and their lessons don't have to stop when it rains.

Reader 2: The people in his village were so happy that they gave their school a new name. They named it after the day the peace deal was signed: the 4th of April School. The name is a great reminder that everyone needs to work together to keep the peace, even

though they might have been on different sides
during the war. This is what Eduardo says:

Reader 3: I like school more now and go every day. It's
important to go, so I can find a job when I'm older.
I want to have peace, not war. Now there's peace
it feels safer at home and we won't have to run
away again.

4. Stress that Eduardo's community named the school after the
day the peace deal was signed because peace is so important
to them. Ask the children why they think the school and
peace are important to Eduardo. What do they think has
changed for him since they have had peace and his school was
repaired?

 ## Time for reflection

Close your eyes.
Imagine how it would feel if rain was pouring down on us or the
hot sun was beating down and dust was blowing in our faces.
Now imagine what school is like for Eduardo now that there is
peace and his school has been repaired. How would it feel to be
sitting in his classroom? What sounds can you hear? Is this what
we think peace sounds like?

 ## Prayer

Let's think about all the children in the world who are caught up
in war.

We pray for peace in these countries so that all children will
be able to play and go to school without fear.

Let's think about how we can all do our bit to keep the peace.
Think about someone you've had an argument with recently.
Remember to make it up with them today.

We pray that we will have the strength to find a peaceful way
to end arguments in the future.
Amen.

Now shake hands with the person beside you, as a sign of peace.

Class activities

1 How do we feel?

Ask the children to remember an argument they have had. How did they feel before and after they made up? List their feelings on the board.

Reread Eduardo's story. Point out that the fighting in Angola was so serious that Eduardo's family had to leave their home. How do they think this made Eduardo feel? Make a list of these feelings.

How must he feel now that the war is over? Make another list of Eduardo's feelings.

Children could write a poem using the feeling words on the board. It could be about Eduardo's experiences or their own.

Ask them to draw an image representing themselves on the left-hand side of a piece of paper and an image representing Eduardo on the right-hand side, then write 'feeling words' against the two images. Put words that apply to both images in the middle, and more person-specific words towards the appropriate edge.

PSHE, English

2 Rebuilding after conflict

Remind the children of how they thought the war made Eduardo feel. Explain that war destroys buildings and amenities (things like schools and hospitals), as well as lives. Name some amenities and ask children to raise their hands if they've used them recently: school, health centre, railway station, bus stop, shops, etc.

Ask the children how losing these things might have made life hard for Eduardo. Eduardo drew a picture at school of the mountains near where he lives. Ask half the class to draw a scene showing what Eduardo might have drawn during the war, and half to draw a scene showing what Eduardo might draw now that there is peace in Angola.

Display the 'before' and 'after' pictures in pairs and talk about the differences. As a class, discuss how much happier life is when people live in peace.

PSHE, English (structured talking), Citizenship

3 Dealing with feelings

Explain that although the war is over, there are still problems. Parents of children in Eduardo's class fought against each other during the war. How might this affect how they get on with each other now? As a class make a list of the things that children at Eduardo's school might need to do to make sure they get on with each other: for example, not judging others because of the 'side' their parents were on; making an effort to get on with everyone; thinking carefully about what they say and how it might affect other people.

Ask the children to think again about an argument they have had. Ask them in pairs to tell each other how they sorted it out. Ask the partners to tell the class about how the conflict was resolved.

PSHE, English, Citizenship

4 Solving problems together

Ask each pair to join with another and think of as many ways as possible of solving an argument. One person from each group should feed back to the class. Write the answers on the board. Are any of the ideas similar to the suggestions the class made about how children at Eduardo's school can live peacefully together?

PSHE, English

5 Ideas for drama

Create 'before' and 'after' still pictures (tableaux made by adopting positions like a freeze frame) showing:

- Life for Eduardo before peace/after peace.
- An argument or conflict at school/the peaceful resolution.
- War/peace.

Create a motivational video using the ideas the children have developed about how to get on with people and resolve conflict: 'The three-step conflict resolution plan – make a big difference to your life in three easy steps'. This can be produced as a live drama, a podcast or a vodcast.

English, IT, Drama

LANDMINE HERO

Suitable for KS2

 ### Aims

To consider the idea of heroes; to learn something about the scourge of landmines and how they can be tackled.

 ### Preparation and materials

- Place 12 pieces of card around the front of the assembly space. On the underside of four of them write 'YOU LOSE' – it is important that the writing cannot be seen when the card is placed face down. It is vital that you know where the four 'YOU LOSE' cards are placed.
- You will need something that makes a loud noise, such as a bell or a rattle – loud enough to make the children jump but not so loud as to cause discomfort.

 ### Assembly

1. Say that you are going to begin with a game and ask for four volunteers. The game is that they each, in turn, have to cross from one side of the space to the other, treading on any four pieces of card. As soon as the first person to cross treads on one of the marked cards, make the loud noise. Show them the underside, and explain that they're out. If anyone makes it across without stepping on any 'YOU LOSE' cards, remove the cards that they used, to make the game harder for the next person. Hopefully the first loud noise will have created an atmosphere of tension that will add to the game.
2. Ask your participants to sit down. Explain that the game was fun and only slightly scary if the loud noise made you jump or nervous. But the game has a serious point. Can anyone think of situations where stepping in the wrong place could lead to

death or some terrible injury such as losing a limb? Accept all suggestions, such as scorpions, snakes, stonefish, falling off a cliff, down a mineshaft, but then focus in on landmines.

Explain that landmines are especially dangerous. They are put in the ground in wartime, but even after a war is over they are still there and will explode if someone, often a child, steps on them, even years later.

3. Tell Ram Chamreun's story:

My name is Ram Chamreun and I live in an area of Cambodia called Kompong Thom. My country was at war for a long time until 1991. Even after the war had stopped, fighting continued for a few more years. The fighting was between the government and a group called the Khmer Rouge, which wanted to be in power. During the war I was a soldier in the government army.

I managed to survive the war without getting seriously hurt, but on the way back from a patrol one day I stepped on a landmine. I heard it go bang but didn't realize I had lost my leg – I just thought it had been cut. When I realized what had happened I went into shock. I was taken into hospital.

At first, they gave me a wooden leg. It was very difficult to use and it really hurt. Now I have an artificial limb, which fits just under my knee. It's so much better now.

I'm not a soldier any more. I now work for an organization called the Mines Advisory Group (MAG). My job is to help get rid of the landmines in Cambodia. There are so many landmines left behind after the war that every month lots of people are killed or injured by them. There are about 500 of us who do this work. We are called de-miners. Many of the de-miners used to be soldiers like me, but now we want to help save people's lives. We have been trained to clear the landmines.

People keep telling me that my job is very dangerous, but I'm not scared. MAG trained me very well and I follow their safety rules. I enjoy my work and I think it is very important. Without this work it would be unsafe for people to walk to the well to get water, or to go to school, or to farm the land. I just want to help people in my community to live their lives without the danger of losing limbs or being killed by landmines.

4. Ask questions about the story.

- What job does Ram Chamreun now do?
- What job did he do before?
- Do you think what he does is dangerous?
- Why does he do it?

5. Stress the importance of training and following the safety rules. Explain that even today in the UK and Ireland people still find explosives from the Second World War, which ended over 60 years ago. But in some countries like Cambodia landmines are much more common.
6. Do you think Ram Chamreun and his fellow workers are heroes? What makes them heroes?

 Time for reflection

Ram Chamreun is a local hero. He is working for his community and helping to save many lives. But he thinks he is just an ordinary person.

Think about how you are special and what you can do to help those in your community here at school. There may also be things we can do to help people like Ram Chamreun in other parts of the world. We are all special ... we can all be heroes.

If appropriate, include the following readings:

> Then the King will say to those on his right, 'Come, you who are blessed by my Father; take your inheritance, the kingdom prepared for you since the creation of the world. For I was hungry and you gave me something to eat, I was thirsty and you gave me something to drink, I was a stranger and you invited me in, I needed clothes and you clothed me, I was sick and you looked after me, I was in prison and you came to visit me.' (Bible, Matthew 25.34–36, NIV)

The actions of each of us, human or nonhuman, have contributed to the world in which we live. We all have a common responsibility for our world and are connected with everything in it. (His Holiness the 14th Dalai Lama)

Prayer

Thank you for ordinary people who are heroes, like Ram Chamreun.
Help me to become an everyday hero –
someone who does good things for those around me.
Amen.

Class activities

1 Ram Chamreun's story

Recap the story of Ram Chamreun. Talk about the kinds of questions children would like to ask Ram. Carry out a 'hot seating' activity: teacher and children take it in turns to be Ram Chamreun. Leave the list of questions on display for children to add to at a later time.

English, Drama, PSHE, Geography

2 Everyday activities

As a class, talk about the many things that the children do every day: get up, have breakfast, go to school, play games with friends, walk or run around, hobbies and sports, eating and drinking. Talk about how everyday life where Ram Chamreun lives is different and often very dangerous.

Ask the children to suggest the similarities and differences between their everyday activities and the same activities in Cambodia. For example, for some children it is dangerous to walk to school because of landmines. In the UK and Ireland it is generally safe to walk to school but there are sometimes dangers from busy roads and traffic. People can get safe drinking water from a tap. In Cambodia people often have to walk to a well to get their water, and landmines can even make it dangerous to collect water.

PSHE, Geography

3 **A day in the life**
Talk about the difference Ram Chamreun's work makes to
his community. Ask children to imagine that they live in
Ram Chamreun's area. They could write an account or
produce a cartoon strip of a day in their life before Ram
Chamreun was trained to do his work and a day in their life
since he has started to clear landmines.

English, Citizenship

4 **Research**
Working in groups, the children can undertake research on
landmines. See if they can answer these questions:

- Which countries have a major problem with landmines?
- Which UK celebrity who died over ten years ago is partly
  remembered for her work on raising awareness of the
  problem of landmines?
- How many landmines do the authorities think are still in
  the ground in Cambodia or one of the other countries you
  have researched?
- How many deaths and serious injuries are there each year
  from landmines?
- What can people in the UK do about this problem?

They can present their findings as a display, a written and
illustrated report or in a follow-on assembly.

Study skills, English, PSHE, Citizenship

WAR AND THE FAMILY

Suitable for KS2

 Aims

To bring into focus the reality of war and its effect on families

 Preparation and materials

- Rehearse three children to read the parts of the Diab family: Zainab (mother), Ali (father), and Wujdan (ten-year-old girl). Two other children take the non-speaking parts of Wujdan's younger brothers.

 Assembly

1. Ask about war-based films and stories and/or computer games with which the children are familiar. Talk about the exciting moments, moments of tension and fear or last-minute escapes and also about defence against, and attacks on, 'the enemy'.

   Explain that the children are going to hear an ordinary family talk about the way that war has affected them. They're a family from Lebanon, which shares a border with Israel. In 2006, Israeli soldiers, tanks and aeroplanes attacked Lebanon after two Israeli soldiers were kidnapped on a border patrol.

2. Introduce the Diab family one by one, asking them to step forward as you say their names: Ali Diab is the father of the family, he is a tailor; Zainab is the mother; and they have three children: Wujdan (girl) who is ten years old; and two boys: Melham is seven and Hammoudi is just five years old. Let's hear from them:

Zainab: Our house was hit twice during the war. We didn't hear the planes but we could hear the missiles hitting the ground. Everything would become covered in an orange light and then there was a huge explosion. The important thing is that we are all alive. The first bombardment caused a lot of rubble and rocks to be dropped and our car was destroyed by flying rocks. Shrapnel destroyed our cooker and there was damage to the kitchen. During the war everybody left the village except us. We didn't have money to leave so we had to stay in the house. My parents came to stay with us and we were all sleeping in the same room. I was afraid the walls would cave in ... nine of us in one room. Hammoudi was shaking like a bird and he would hide under his father's shirt. In this village 170 homes were destroyed or damaged.

Ali: We feared for the lives of our children. Anger was also a natural feeling we had; but the first feeling was one of fear for our children. The first bombardment was three missiles and in the second bombing there were four very large missiles, which weigh a tonne each.

Wujdan: I'm ten years old and in the fourth grade at school. My favourite subject is Arabic. We play football at school – the girls and boys play separately. My favourite game is 'catch' with a ball. Hammoudi says that I was scared when the bombs fell but I wasn't, because my mum and dad were there. I was shocked. I'm happy that it's over. I don't think there will be another war again.

Zainab: Now there is nowhere safe for the children to play. No playgrounds, no music. Our children just play in the street, in the road, and they throw stones at each other for fun. Melham injured his head when someone threw a large stone at him. I don't like living this way.

3. Explain that there are two children who you haven't heard from. You want to ask the watching children for their ideas about what seven-year-old Melham and five-year-old Hammoudi would say, now that you have heard some of their family's story. Move to each child in turn and ask for ideas about what they would say. Value all contributions and at the end you could ask the two children being Melham and Hammoudi for their views.

4. Point out that this is just an ordinary family, caught up in war. No one in the family died but they were all frightened and their house and car were seriously damaged. Real life war is very different from how we see it in films and games and for ordinary people it can be terrifying and make a mess of their lives.

After the war the Diab family received help from charities through a local organization, which is good but that money and support could have gone elsewhere if there had been no war in the first place!

Time for reflection

Think about the Diab family: Zainab, Ali, Wujdan, Melham and Hammoudi.
Just an ordinary family caught up in war.
Wujdan said: 'I was shocked. I'm happy that it's over.'
Zainab said: 'Hammoudi was shaking like a bird and he would hide under his father's shirt.'
Ali said: 'We feared for the lives of our children.'
Think about how war affected this ordinary family.

Prayer

Dear God,
We pray for the Diab family and for all victims of war,
ordinary families caught up in battles and conflicts between politicians and armies.
We pray for peace across our divided world
and we pray that we may learn to be peacemakers.
Amen.

Class activities

1 Story – when the bombs came

Write a story based on what you have heard about the Diab family. In your story show what happens to an ordinary family caught up in war. Try to express the emotions that the family experience, using a variety of feeling words such as 'fear', 'nervous', 'anxious', 'anger'.

English

2 Current wars

Where in the world are there conflicts and war at the moment? In groups, children can pick a conflict, research it and explain it to the rest of the class:

- Who is fighting and why?
- How did the conflict start?
- How long has it been going on?
- What do you think could bring an end to the conflict?

Discuss these conflicts with the children, and try to present both sides.

Research, Presentation skills, English

3 Peace and conflict at school

Discuss any conflicts that have occurred in the school. How were they resolved? Why is it sometimes difficult to be peaceful? What does it mean to the children to be peaceful? What sorts of things can the children think of that prevent peace (on a global scale and in school)?

PSHE, Citizenship

4 Peace words and symbols

The class could find out how to say 'peace' in different languages. They could explore different symbols that convey peace.

PSHE, Citizenship

Section 5
Environmental issues

CILLA RECYCLED!

Suitable for Whole School

Aims

To reinforce the importance of recycling as a way of combating climate change and creating a fairer world.

Preparation and materials

- You may prefer to use the story in class prior to the assembly, or to split it in two, spreading it across two assemblies. The story is told by 'Cilla' so a female voice is best.

Assembly

1. Introduce and read the story, asking the children to listen carefully to see if they can work out who Cilla is and what she is talking about!

Cilla's story*
Ouch! Don't bump so! I know you can't help it but it's the same every morning. You're the worst, Edgy, with those sharp edges. Oh, I can't wait to get to school and get out of here and into the light. I wonder what it'll be today. A story, I hope – I love telling stories – well, writing them really because that's what I do.

I'm Cilla. Penny Pen says it's because I'm sillier than the average pencil, but I know I'm Cilla because I'm Pencilla – a pencil, you see, and Penny Pen's a ... she's a pen, obviously. Then there's Paddy, he's a notepad, Edgy the ruler and of course we're all wrapped up in Casey – the pencil case. And I can ...

Whoa ... he's started to run – must be late. Ouch – do mind out, Edgy, honestly! We're all in Simon's backpack on the way to school and every morning he dawdles along until the last minute and then he has to run like crazy. No consideration for us at all. Oh no, we're just thrown around like so much rubbish – anyone would think we didn't have feelings at all.

We're here, in the playground. He's made it, thank goodness for that! And he's got a few minutes to spare. So as long as he doesn't jump about too much I can tell you about the strange dream I had last night. At least I think it was a dream. I was dozing happily in Casey the case – which is where I live when Simon's not using me to make up a fantastic story or do a terrific drawing. So there I was, half-asleep and half-awake, and it seemed to me that I remembered something ...

I was in the dark. I wasn't alone, there were lots of my friends there, and they were all piled up on top of me. Then I heard these strange clinking and clicking sounds. I was just thinking, 'That's odd,' when ... whoa ... I was sliding down a chute. It was actually quite good fun.

I was getting to enjoy it when ... Ouch! I landed with a bump and suddenly it was blinding light, like I'd just come out of a dark tunnel. But before I had a chance to take it all in ... I suddenly felt all warm on the inside.

What a strange dream – I mean, what was that all about? When I told the others they all thought it was just a silly dream. As Casey said, 'You're a pencil, Cilla, how on earth could all that have happened to you?' They laughed at me, but a strange thing happened a bit later because Penny told me that she had a funny dream memory too.

She remembered writing lots of words, which isn't unusual as she is a pen, but she said they all came out very fast in very straight lines, not like they were written at all, · and they had a sort of buzzy rat-a-tat-tat sound ...

What do you make of that – how could a pen remember something like that?

Oh, there's the school bell; it's time to go in. I do hope we have stories to write today. Here we go, into the classroom and Miss Baptiste is taking the register. It's not fair, really; I mean, our names never get called, do they? Only Simon and his classmates. Oh, listen a minute, she's telling them what they'll be working on, let's hope it's a story.

It's very hard to hear in here, but I think she said something about cheese Vikings. Maybe we're doing the history of dairy produce; or maybe it was bee-fighting – do bees do that? I don't know. If Simon would hurry up and take Casey out of his backpack, and take me out of Casey, we might get somewhere.

Oh, hang on, I think I heard something about tree-cycling. That sounds a bit dangerous, especially going up the trunk – you'd have to go very fast. Oh, that reminds me, Casey once told me that he used to go very fast. 'Oh yes,' he said, 'in my younger days I used to zoom along, 50, 60, 70 miles an hour sometimes. I'd whiz round and round like a spinning top, faster and faster.' None of us dared ask him how he, a humble pencil case, could go so fast. If we did, he'd probably clip us with his zip and tell us to be quiet. But isn't that odd, you see? Casey's got a funny dream memory just like me and Penny. I bet Paddy the notebook has one too if we could just get him to open up.

At last, we're out. Hello world, hello classroom, hello everybody. Now, what's Miss Baptiste written on the board? Is it cheese Vikings, bee-fighting or tree-cycling? Oh, it's none of them, it's recycling. I suppose that's all about riding your bike the same way every day. Sounds pretty boring.

Oh wait, must pay attention, Simon's picked me up to use me. Here we go, I'm writing:

'Recycling is a way of making better use of all the world's resou … rescource … '

Oh, he's crossing out …

' … all the things in the world because lots of things, like plastic, which is made from oil, will run out if we don't make better use of them.'

A pause, he's thinking. That's quite interesting, isn't it? So instead of throwing things away you use them again – clever. Oh, he's writing again.

'Some things, like single-use cameras, can just be used again, but other things are melted down and made into new things. A good example would be plastic bottles, which can be made into new bottles or other things.'

Well, I never – that is fascinating. Now he's writing a heading down – better concentrate.

'An example of recycling in my life.'

Well, I wonder what he's going to write. I know he used one of his dad's best shirts as a painting apron but I don't think that counts. Oh, here we go. He's writing fast, like he knows all about it.

'My best example of recycling is my pencil case and all the things in it.'

What?

'The case is made from recycled car tyres, the notebook from car tyres and recycled paper, the pen is made from recycled computer printers ... '

But ... that explains everything! Casey's memory of going fast – he did go fast, he was a car tyre! And Penny was made from old computer printers so no wonder she remembers writing fast in straight lines. But what about me? Come on, Simon, write about me!

'And this very pencil I'm writing with is made from ... '

Yes, come on!

'... old plastic drinks cups from vending machines.'

Old cups! I'm just an old throwaway cup! The cheek of it. Oh, he's finishing off:

'So it has served two useful purposes already. But, best of all, this pencil has helped to conserve some of the world's precious oil. So it is very special.'

Well, if you put it like that ... I'm a hero, and I write stories. Not bad for a pencil that was once a cup in a drinks machine, eh?

2. Talk about the story, recapping which recycled products the characters were made from:

- Pencil case: recycled car tyres.
- Notebook: recycled car tyres and recycled paper.
- Pen: recycled computer printers.
- Pencil: recycled plastic drinks cups from vending machines.

3. Talk about recycling and why it is important: include the children's own examples of recycling. If you have done other assemblies around development issues, ask the children how recycling can be related to development.

   Explain that the world only has a limited amount of the fuels that we mostly use for powering our transport and creating the energy that we use. So we need to recycle as many things as we can to help look after the world's dwindling resources.

4. That's one reason, but there's another urgent reason why we need to recycle. Find out what the children know about greenhouse gases and climate change. Point out that climate change is hitting the developing world hard, with a risk of increased flooding and drought, but the developing world has not created the problem. So all of us need to save energy and recycle as much as possible. Challenge the children to recycle more waste and to seek out and use recycled products, like those in the story.

 Time for reflection

We throw away so much every day: food wrappers, plastic bottles, paper …
What do you throw away each day?
How much do you recycle?
Will you take up the challenge to recycle more, and to seek out and use recycled products?

 Prayer

Dear God,
It's a wonderful world,
with so much for us to use and enjoy.
Please help us to be good citizens of the world,
to recycle more and to use more recycled products.
Amen.

Class activities

1 Audit

Conduct an audit of recycling in school. Which classes have the best record and how can all classes improve their recycling? What is the best way to present the results?

Citizenship, PSHE, Maths

2 Comic strip

The children can rewrite the story of Cilla as a comic strip, splitting it among the class so that children do either (a) the journey to school; (b) Cilla's dream; (c) Casey's dream; or (d) the end of the story. They will need to think about:

- How will you portray the different characters?
- Break down the story so that you know how many frames you will need.
- Identify the most important or exciting parts of the story and give them larger or more interesting frames (a different shape or a coloured border, for example).
- How will you represent the dreams?

English, Art and design

3 Research

Find out about local and national recycling schemes. The children can choose one and prepare a presentation on it for the rest of the class (this could be a small group activity). The presentation should include:

- A clear description of the scheme and what it aims to achieve.
- Some statistics showing how successful it is.
- Their view of the scheme and suggestions for improvement.
- Time for questions from the audience.

Research skills, English

4 Development and recycling

What is the link between development work (helping developing countries to help themselves) and recycling? Can the children create a pictorial representation linking:

- recycling
- greenhouse gases
- dwindling resources
- climate change
- development issues?

Research skills, English, Citizenship, Art and design

WIDER, WIDER RIVER

Suitable for Whole School

 ### Aims

To understand the effects of erosion on communities.

 ### Preparation and materials

- This is one of two linked assemblies based on the experience of a Bangladeshi boy, ten-year-old Sagor. This assembly concentrates on his experiences of erosion and the next assembly, **Sweet or Salty**, focuses on the effects of climate change.
- You will need an opaque container of water. The water should be dirty, but this should not be apparent at first so perhaps use a lid to keep the contents fully hidden.
- You will need a clear glass to pour the muddy water into.
- A table to put the water container on so that the sitting children can see it. The table needs to be small and light, as it has to be moved progressively across the space.
- Read through or prepare some children to read Sagor's story.

 ### Assembly

1. Take your opaque container of water and place it on the table at the far end of the space. Ask how many steps it will take to reach it from where you are at the front of the assembly space. Take suggestions and ask for a volunteer to come and stand where you are. Ask them to take the paces when you say 'go', and we'll see if they were right about the distance.

   Count down, three, two, one ... but as you do so, walk to the table with the container on it, pick up the table and move it forward, so that the volunteer goes too far and ends up in the wrong place! Don't let the volunteer cheat in any way – they must stick to the agreed number of paces.

2. Repeat the process, taking suggestions for the new number of steps. Again, move the cup and table so that the volunteer misses. Repeat several times, ensuring each time that the volunteer misses. Thank your volunteer and ask them to sit down.

3. Ask everyone to remember what they've just seen while they listen to these words of Sagor, a ten-year-old boy from Bangladesh.

> My name is Sagor. I'm ten years old and study in class three. The best five things in my life are to study, to fish, to play football and cricket, and play chase with my friends.
>
> I like to study, it's fun. I especially like grammar books. It takes me about 15 minutes to get to my school. When it rains it's muddy for half the way and the other half is OK, but there is a proper concrete road coming soon.
>
> I was born here, but in my life I have seen our first house washed away by the river. And the river is coming to erode us a second time. My old house was about 300 hands (about 100 metres) away from where the river is now.
>
> The river has closed in on us. I don't think our house will be here in the next few years. It's not a good feeling. I don't feel good when I think that the river will come and take it away. My parents worry a lot. I also worry a little.

4. Thank your readers and ask everyone what they think the connection is between the game you just played and Sagor's story. Discuss the idea that the river is moving nearer to Sagor's house – it is getting wider. Talk about erosion. What is it, what causes it? Then ask the children to listen to what Sagor thinks is causing the erosion:

> I think there are two major reasons why the riverbank is eroding. The first is when the big ships and army boats go on the river, it makes a lot of waves, which break the side of the river and when the sides break the river gets bigger. The other reason is that the police come and chase people and do

not let them fish. This also causes waves which beat the sides, so the river gets bigger.

5. So Sagor's home is in danger again. Now explain that the river water is not good to drink. It is muddy and carries disease, but there is no other clean, healthy water supply nearby. Show the muddy water in your container by pouring it into a clear glass. That's why charities work through local organizations to help people like Sagor and his community to get clean water. But this won't stop the erosion; that will take a big effort and time.

Sagor is hopeful for the future, though. He says: 'When I grow up I want to be a doctor. I want to serve others and serve the poor when they are sick.'

 ## Time for reflection

Water: clean and bright,
Cool and just right.
When you're thirsty or hot,
You can drink down a lot.
Water is always there,
To drink and to share.

But not everyone has the water we do.
It doesn't always flow gushing and free.
Some people are thirsty, their mouths dry too.
In a world of plenty, how can this be?

 ## Prayer

Dear God,
Thank you for the gift of water,
the sparkling, flowing water of life.
We pray for those who do not have enough to drink.
We pray that in a world of plenty we will work together so
that no one need be thirsty.
Amen.

Class activities

1 Lists and categories

List all the things that we use water for and then sort them into categories. Categories might include: cold drinks, hot drinks, cooking, leisure, travel, exercise.

English

2 Collage

Create a class collage on the theme of water. Include examples of the many uses of water as well as its scarcity in some parts of the world.

Art

3 Story

Write a story in which water plays a major part. It can be about anything connected with water: a boat trip, a seaside adventure, a thirsty day, a plant that you forget to water, or a day in the life of someone like Sagor. See how many different water stories the class can come up with and use these to illustrate the centrality of water in our lives.

English

4 Water use

We are not usually short of water in the UK and Ireland, but we still need to be careful how we use it. Can the children come up with ways of saving water at home and at school? For example, turning taps off when brushing teeth, taking showers instead of baths, using waste water to water plants and so on. Can they design posters to get this important message across?

PSHE, Citizenship, Art and design

SWEET OR SALTY

Suitable for Whole School

Aims

To examine one effect of climate change in a Bangladeshi community.

Preparation and materials

- This is the second of two linked assemblies based on the experiences of Sagor, a ten-year-old Bangladeshi boy.
- You will need two jugs of water, one with a small amount of salt mixed in. You will need to know which is which but it should not be obvious to the participating children.
- Some glasses/plastic cups for tasting the water.

Assembly

1. Begin by recapping Sagor's story from the **Wider, wider river** assembly, or briefly introduce it if you haven't yet used it.
2. Say that you have some more information about water today and you want to begin with an experiment. Ask for a volunteer to take a sip of each of the two waters. Stress that they should only sip but without explaining why (you don't want them to be ill!). What do they notice about the taste? If they can't identify the salty taste, ask someone else to have a go until you arrive at the fact that the water in one of the jugs tastes salty.
3. Talk about salt water: it's good for preserving foods (brine); many things are cooked in salted water – vegetables, rice and pasta, for example; and we all need a certain amount of salt in our diet to keep us healthy (although in the UK and Ireland most of us have too much salt). Ask your volunteer what it

tasted like. Would they like to drink salted water all the time? Point out that this would make you very sick, very quickly!

4. Say that Sagor has a problem with salt water and you're going to tell a bit more of his story now. But you need some help with sound effects. Every time you say the word 'salty' you want everyone to say 'Yuk!' and every time you say 'sweet' you want them to make a happy 'Mmmm' sound. Then begin the story.

Sagor and his friends in Bangladesh have always used the river water for washing and sometimes cooking things and even drinking (after boiling of course!). For a long time the water was good to use, Sagor says it was **sweet**. But now the water is often **salty**, not **sweet** but **salty**.

When it's **salty** it can't be used for nearly as many things as when it's **sweet**. So, to put it simply, **sweet** water is good and **salty** water is not! Let's get that message across, shall we? Ready:

> **Sweet**
> **Salty**
> **Salty**
> **Sweet**
>
> (*pause*)
>
> **Swinging** – just to catch you out!

5. Stress that the noise-making part of the assembly is now over and you can say 'sweet' or 'salty' without sound effects from now on! Ask the children what they think could have caused the river water to turn salty. Value all suggestions and work round to the fact that seawater is salty. Ask how seawater might be getting into the river.

6. Talk about climate change, which is caused by global warming. Global warming is causing the sea to warm up, which makes it expand and so the sea levels rise; this is what is causing the salty seawater to find its way into rivers. This is upsetting the balance of life and making the river water too salty for Sagor and his friends to use.

Point out that energy use across the world contributes to climate change because of the carbon dioxide that builds up in the atmosphere. We can all do something about this by using less energy. What ideas do the children have for using less energy at home and at school?

 ## Time for reflection

Think about Sagor and his friends in Bangladesh.
Think about how they can't use the river water as they always used to.
Picture in your mind the sea level rising, and the seawater seeping across the land and into the rivers.
It's a big problem, but we can all do something to help by using less of the energy that causes climate change – what could you do to save energy?

 ## Prayer

Dear God,
We think about everything that we have.
All the technology that we use at home and at school: TVs, computers, games consoles – even simple lights!
We enjoy using them, but please help us to remember to do so sensibly, turning them off when we can to save precious energy.
Amen.

 ## Class activities

1 Energy saving at school
Ask the children to come up with ideas for using less energy at school. Discuss the ideas together and mount a campaign to help put them into action. Elements of the campaign could be:

- Posters and fliers
- An assembly
- A drama/dance production

- A story-writing competition
- A podcast or vodcast.

Science, Art, English, Citizenship

2 Energy saving at home
Ask the children to come up with ideas for using less energy at home. Ask them to keep an energy-saving diary to record all the ways that they save energy over a week.

Science, English

3 Acrostic poem
Ask the children to write an acrostic poem using the word 'WATER' to supply the initial letter of each line. Can they come up with something that uses the themes of this and the previous assembly? For example, the importance of water to life; the ease with which we can obtain water and the difficulties people have in other parts of the world; 'sweet' and 'salty' water; the effects of climate change.

English

4 Estimating water usage
Can the children estimate the amount of water used in school in a day? How would they go about doing this? Can they suggest ways to find out: how much water is drunk in a day (average for each person in the class ... total for each class ... times the number of classes in the school); how much is used in the kitchens (research with dinner staff needed); how much is used in the toilets (counting the number of pupils using the toilets, plus internet research on how much water per flush).

Maths